# Going Live

## By

## Sarah Schmitt

Stefanie, Going Live is just as much yours as it is mine.

Through all of my madness, you've definitely earned this

dedication. My sister, my friend, my rock….thank you.

1

**...and so we begin**

You know that moment you're running way too fast

down a flight of stairs and you hit that second to last

step...you're convinced it's the end. Your heel slides

clumsily off the edge, muscles freeze...your reaching for

a banister that might as well be 100 miles away.

Someone is always standing within eye shot to feel and

sense your incredible fear. You look at one another and

the world becomes a slow motion battle...this is

it...clearly your demise...and you land, stiff as a board and aching only because you froze and never thought for one second, "Jesus Christ, man...it's one step. What's the worst that can happen?" Your friend purses her lips and tries to calmly ask, "Are you ok?" After you've both yelled,"OOOHH" in unison. They know that fear, you know that fear. We've been there a hundred times.....that's life. The moments you know you can't possibly go on...that's it! I GIVE UP...I AM GOING TO SLIDE OFF OF THIS ONE SIX INCH STEP AND IT WILL CLEARLY BE THE LAST STEP I EVER TAKE! But you make it. You land on your feet....and 9 times out of 10, you'll look into the eyes of your frozen, smirking, fighting with all their might not to laugh in your face friend...and crack up.

There is always going to be moments when we think it might be our last...or it "has to be", but there's always a reason to laugh at your slip because that's the moment you're alive.

Listen, I'm 35 years old. I moved back from the backwoods of Texas to my home in Staten Island, NY. I did laundry in my underwear on my back porch that was made of plywood while a one eyed cat I called Jack yelled at me to feed her and her two very homely, wiry newborns while my very velvety, fat, lazy eight cats looked on from the kitchen window. I got hit with a bug I'm sure was made of armor that made me smell like soup for 3 days...they tell me it was a stink bug. Why would the Lord create something called a "stink bug"? Cosmic joke perhaps? I was asked by questionable looking men named Buzz, Cap and Leon if I wanted to try what was cooking in a thousand year old cauldron that had been bubbling in the dead center of a crispy lawn for two weeks. I passed on it...and I'm sorry I never found out how they're concoction tasted. I looked behind me when the cashier said, "how y'all doin'?" because dammit I'm only one woman! When the young lady behind the counter asked me if I was bald, while making my sandwich I looked down at my lap because I know I have hair on my head. "Are YOU Bawld?" "Um, no I don't believe so." (You don't believe so? What is this? Fucking Candid Camera?)"Ugh, fine...here's your sandwich." I'll walk back 2 miles in a 115 degree heat to put mayo on my sandwich because....it was the condiment on my sandwich. Therefore...if I am bald, I don't want mustard or mayo. Dare I hand her back my freshly wrapped meal and ask for a slap of mayo? Admit defeat? Never....I ALWAYS eat painfully dry cold cuts on cardboard bread you silly beast!

Over 100 times in my life I've considered suicide...seriously. But I'd have missed baked beans and first kisses. The first time you slow dance with a crush...a laugh at some witty adult like response from a 4 year old. A blazing orgasm that seems to last almost too long that makes you laugh when you're done. The heat of embarrassment from writing this even though I'm 35, and I know my parents will read that last moment. Pick your moment....I'm nobody special. I'm just some girl sitting in a chair with a notebook. If you want to take my hand and laugh at my moments, so maybe one of yours seems less intense...then my hand is extended. Welcome to my world.

## Chapter 1

I thought about writing a personal ad….in the shower.

Let's face it; all of our best ideas happen in the shower.

So…shower/personal ad If I'm mildly dishonest I'm a 35 year old attractive swgf (for those of you that are not familiar with personal ad jargon because you're happily married or just staring blankly at the letters, then it means single white gay female) Enjoys traveling, the arts, music…you get it blah blah yawn.

Now if I'm honest listen to how sexy I am….try not to knock down the door.

35y/o  sw maybe kinda gay but occasionally has a tussle with a guy friend if he seems to be particularly witty one night and I'm pissed off at how gross and wicked women can be *here's where I get sexy* unemployed, recovering drug addict/alcoholic (kind of), currently living back in my adolescent bedroom in a stifling hot attic at my parents very beautiful, very historic...very haunted house. Don't sweat it though...because I recently painted it from psychotic, I don't know what I was thinking, green to a very romantic burgundy and spent my last unemployment check on fabulous bedding and pillows. I have wonderful matching candles, but my mother won't let me light them. Now my parents will give us privacy, but the floor creeks so no sudden movements and for god's sake, put a pillow over your mouth, you'll get us all thrown out! I recently lost about 70 lbs, so my clothes hang beautifully. Listen...it was either new capris at the midnight sale at Wal-Mart or bedding. I have my priorities in order, and there are such things as belts. I don't have a car, but I can ask my mom if I can borrow her whip, and pick you up, but I gotta be

home by midnight, and I cannot have one single drink.

Yes, I'm on Facebook, but I can only go on in intervals of

5 minutes every 4 hours because my mother is addicted

to Farmville and Bejeweled Blitz and starts to shake if I

take too much time. My father won't give up his

password on his laptop because he's a government spy

or thinks I'm a hacker because I can maneuver Google

like a king and he doesn't want me to find out how he

secretly uses Youtube to hear music because he thinks

it's some form of stealing. I'd love to take you out for a

romantic dinner, but you'll have to settle for a tea light

candle at Wendy's unless I managed to get to the penny

arcade at the bank and then maybe we can hit Denino's

for a pitcher ONE PITCHER of sangria and a pizza. If I hit

the couch cushions and junk drawers, I might be able to

buy you a small ice at Ralph's, but I'll let you know.

Ready to propose to me yet? Get this....

I used to be a very successful private investigator...even had paparazzi ask me a question that warranted a "no comment" response. I ran a company. Had a beautiful, intelligent, very intense workaholic for a girlfriend, the most amazing "In-laws" for the most part. I had a beautiful home and one being built. I wore designer clothes and I was always tan...I'm not quite sure why, but I was indeed always tan. I had money in my pocket, powerful wit on my side...brilliance in my field. I was a likeable boss I think and a decent partner in life...I took 52 Percocet a day. After 6 o'clock, I washed that down with a pint of Southern Comfort and a six pack of Corona. Sorry, no. They were Coronitas. The little bottles (I don't want you to think I'm a glutton or anything) I woke up in bed, covered in paint and blood….why?

Because, I apparently became the tool guy when I

blacked out. I made love once every three months and it

didn't bother me one bit physically because I couldn't

feel a damn thing anyway. It bothered me

emotionally...because I loved her and I knew I was failing

her. Is this the moment I die? What to do? Maybe hang

myself?


Then I would have missed the first time I saw the love of

my life….and felt like heaven brought itself to me

instead.

## Chapter 2

"Sarah….are you in the shower?" *water running*"Yes dad…do you need to get in here?""No, I just heard the water running, and I was wondering if anyone was in there?" *blank stare only interrupted by shampoo racing down into my very wide eyes…I got nothing.

Living with my parents again is quite an experience. My father likes to talk…a lot, and my mother likes to pretend she's deaf, but I'm on to her. My father talks in the shower, talks while he's shaving…he talks while he's sitting at the kitchen table eating his 476th egg because someone on the radio told him it was healthy. "Dad, eggs are very high in cholesterol. You might want to slow down on your intake. ". "It's ok…I'm making egg salad."(Good thinking….slop a heaping spoonful of mayo

12

goodness, that'll lower your cholesterol nicely? Can I get you a pint glass of eggnog or would you like to just stick with whole chocolate milk?) Anyway...he talks. No matter where he is or who's around...he's chatting away. But I will tell you this....if you whisper lightly at any time of day or night, in any corner of this enormous house, "Dad, what's a 10 letter word for stinky?", before you finish your thought he'll shout malodorous like he's been waiting his whole life for you to ask him that question. He's eternally 16 with the wisdom of a 60 year old man. He's just completely lost the ability to have an inner monologue, and we enjoy the benefits of some very colorful, seemingly impossible to understand epitaphs. He will always follow up with a resounding, "Ya know, Tri (short for Patricia), Sar?" Now here is where my mother feigns "deafness" and she'll swear to you on all that is good and holy that she truly cannot hear. Rattle her bag to remove a miniscule xanax after a particularly shitty day and she'll fly through room like Wonder Woman and just give you "the eye". My mother is my rock and the vault that holds all my secrets. She stands in front of me so no one can see I'm down. I've also discovered if I follow up quietly with a "faggot", she'll always turn and say, "I'm not the faggot in this house, Sarah!" That's how I know she's faking her hearing impairment. Offensive words and meds always seem to command a response.

*A quick word of caution to the reader: You'll come to find out quickly that I refuse to have truly linear thoughts. You're entering a certifiable mind. Good luck!*

**True conversation with my doctor**

I'm breaking my own HIPAA rule:

"Listen, I think I'm going to stop taking this medication. I think it's making me nauseous. I can't deal with this every day. I have a life...and it's seizure medication. I don't have seizures. I've never had a seizure. Honestly, I don't even know what it's for?"

"It, um....helps with anxiety. You told me specifically no benzos. This was an alternative."

"Ok, well that was 400 years ago. Safe to say....I've worked on the anxiety. I'm ready to stop this stuff. I really think it's making me feel sick."

"Ok, well....Sarah, you can't just stop taking that particular medication because in some patients, after missing a day, they broke out with some type of blood rash and died within 3 days."

*very very long silent pause*

"You gave me a medication...for my anxiety....that would make me break out into a "blood rash" whatever the fuck (yes, I said the f word) that is...and KILL ME IN 3 DAYS???!!! This is not like leaving the iron on, man? Or not unplugging a curling iron (yes, I said curling iron...because clearly I use a curling iron every day)...Who the hell remembers to do something every single day without fail? What does this thing look like?!!! I don't remember if I even took it today?! What if I missed it today?! I might have missed today. I'm SURE I MISSED TODAY!!!! Did I miss today?!"

"Sarah, calm down. If you missed today...just go back home and take it."

"I work 2 and a half hours from home you ninny (called my doctor a ninny, yes)." "Well, why don't you carry them with you if you know you could get this blood rash....." "Listen, if you say blood rash to me one more time....*deep breath in* let me get this right....this is the medication you gave me...was to help me....with my anxiety?! Well...Doctor....it's not working"

**You can name this chapter whatever you like....**

About 2 years ago, I went to a psychic. I'm not crazy about the idea because I didn't want it to interfere with my own spirituality but, a friend of mine wanted to go, so we went. It was about 2 in the morning. It was clearly before I got sober, so I was hammered and on cough medicine and probably a few other beautiful things that should make you collapse. So here we are, drunk and silly, ringing the bell of a psychic above a women's clothing store. A heavy Dracula like accent asks us to please come up. Well, here's this hot Dracula woman in a long silk nightgown and she's clearly freezing to death. HEADLIGHTS! She's chain smoking, which makes us chain smoke. Now I'm on cough medicine, which was actually because I was sick and I needed it so, to light one cigarette with the last one you smoked felt awesome. She sits on the floor. Now, she starts telling my friend about the regular bullshit...you're going to change your life, I see blonde hair in your future, and

18

you have a nose blah blah. The whole time she's doing this, she's shooting me dirty looks. Finally, she interrupts my friend's fantastic, "you used to have a pet" reading, and says, "You know you're possessed? You know there's a demon inside of you. We need to exorcise this beast within." So I'm feeling pretty good about myself. I'm feeling kinda special and fantastic. I'm looking at this woman and I'm thinking...are my eyes red? Do I have horns I don't know about? So what do I do? I lean forward and growl, Yes I kknnoowwww. She begins, and this is all true, to crawl backwards away from me. So I'm feeling even prettier. I know my friend is aggravated because she wanted to know if she'd ever win the lottery? If she'd ever get a pony for Christmas? Will her dickhole husband decide to take off for Turks and Caicos and stay there? But Dracula stays focused and very visibly afraid. Of course I'm thinking, "is this bitch for real?" Now we start doing this little dance. I'm playing into this game because of course you know what's next. Another money trip. Get this. The way to exorcise "the devil" because we've graduated to Satan once again being who's supposedly inside of me is as follows: So remember I'm half in the bag. Had I not been drunk, I probably would have really gotten upset but instead I begin to hiss and make crazy eyes so she looks more afraid. Ok...I digress...the way to exorcise Beelzebub...pay attention now....is to stand on wet, white paper towels while she chants at me. But I have to make an appointment to come back to stand on the towels. She can't do it tonight because I'm under the influence. Come back Wednesday and we'll rip that demon right outta you! Hhmmmmm....can't I just throw some Bounty on the kitchen floor and put Enigma on or something? "No....I have to do this. You know that you are taken over!" Ugh...I'm not free on Wednesday...think we could contact Lucifer on Friday? "Um, yeah, Friday works." So basically, it's ok for me hang onto my demon for 6 days. Considering he's hanging out swimming around in my blood currently, I suppose it would be ok to feed him cereal for another week. How much is this towel thing gonna cost me, Dracula?

""Um....hmmmm....let me see...* Begins to mumble like she's counting down the things she's going to need to perform the power of Christ compels you! Vell...because you are seeck, I vill knock off de price of de paper towvel. For all of thees...$632.00. Eet eez very important dat you get dees." $632.00 huh? Where'd you pull that beauty? What's the 2 bucks? You said you were knocking off the towvels?! Well listen, I can't pay that much money for wetting my feet and standing on paper towels. Oh yeah, your feet have to be wet. She needs to check how my "prints sit". By the time she finishes blank staring at my prints, she's going to tell me that not only Satan but the hounds of hell, verevolves, all larger gargoyle species and Jimmy Hoffa are possessing me, so Jimmy Hoffa's gonna be an extra $16 because nobody knows where he is. The fact that I have him is newsworthy. I can see Dracula holding up my wet feet and explaining that one. Anyway, I continue to growl and scowl at her and quite honestly, she genuinely looked afraid. I nonchalantly paid the, I don't know, I guess it was about $300.00 total she muscled out of me for telling my friend, "I see you taking a shower....tomorrow....and you vill...vash you hair!" and for telling me Dante's Inferno lives in my small intestines. As we get up to leave, she once again backs away from me and as she's saying goodbye to my friend while sidelong glancing me like I was going to blindside her with my pitchfork. We walk down the stairs and my friend is mumbling about how she's annoyed because she didn't get the winning numbers and then she realizes, she may or may not be walking with and about to get into a car with the red man. She looks at me a little fearfully and I roll my eyes but internally beg there isn't some truth to this maniacal banter. I decide not to go for Transylvanian chanting.

About a month later I'm out at a bar watching my friend's band play. I'm having some drinks and by some I mean too much and out of the crowd comes Stevie Nicks with black hair. Dramatically like a propeller was blowing wind at her flowing garb. Walks up to me and says, "I need to talk to you. Please come with me." Well, I'm drunk, as usual, so I follow her happily. She pulls me aside and says "there's something wicked behind your eyes. You're in grave danger.....$15.00 please." So, my jaw drops as I hand her my wrinkled bills and I get very upset. Now in my drunken state and I may or may not have been on an eight ball of coke, so I was talking to people a little bit. I was auditioning for an auctioneer position is more like it. I begin to ask people if I look like a serial killer. Now I've come to find, if you ever want the new friends you've made to delete your number from their phone, after you've joined forces to save the world tomorrow while shoveling cocaine up the left nostril (the

24

right one is closed for business because in the frame of maybe an hour and a half, you shoveled enough of that pretty white powder up there to kill at least a small tribe. Ask them if they think you look like you're possessed by the devil. I've come to find people generally don't want to continue to do shots with you after you've asked them if you look evil. And the ones that do are either too drunk or flat out weird.

So now I'm pretty upset. What is behind my eyes that these people see? My friends make fun of me because I'm paranoid. Well....you tell me how you feel after 2 people at different times and places tell you you're possessed by the devil. Not just a demon...THE devil himself. Do I go back to this woman and let her do my feet? Nope...I'm going to church. God will take care of this!

Needless to say, after much thought and reflection....

Had I known paper towels could cure alcoholism and drug addiction, I'd have bought the 24 back at Costco and covered my house. Amazing. They saw the devil in me alright.

Amen

**The chapter of things we don't realize we're saying.**

Fall, falling, fallen in love. I don't know about you but, I've never fell or fallen and not hurt myself. The whole phrase is such a red flag and yet we still give it a shot.

Who the hell made up the word couch?

Why do people really say expresso, expecially, pacific instead of specific?

Why in God's name, in this day and age, do we still say words like retard or retarded? Are grown people still rifling that word as if it's acceptable? After years and years of slaves being referred to as nigger do the 21st century ancestors still call each other that, even more ridiculous is the one white guy who's with a group of black men calling each other "niggas", being able to spew that word out and not have his ass handed to him. I'd ask about faggot, queer, dyke, homo...but I use all of them, because I am all of these things, so in retrospect I suppose if African American youth want to call each other the main offensive word...well then, have at it. Personally, I don't have the balls. While I'm at it...if you are white, do not hold your hand up like you're going to slap five with a black man and say, "what's up brother?" because you look ridiculous. The fact that people still call Koreans, Chinese, Japanese, etc., Oriental? It levels right up there with "colored". Don't do it. Midget is just not ok. By the way, I'd like to reiterate, I find little men (is it still little people, or is it something like vertically challenged or small in stature? I'm not being cruel...so again, if you're looking to attack me, it'll fall on deaf ears) sexy. Yes, I sure do find them sexy." And to wrap it up...chink, kike, spic, gook, egg roll, (I don't know why I made 3 Asian insulting nicknames. I promise if I come up with more about other races, I'll just throw it in at any given moment...if it makes you feel better, I'm a dyke drunk, junkie, homo who's a lush with a penchant for the female world, while getting hammered with some fellow lesbos...ps: I no longer have to refer to myself as a junkie or a drunk but I choose to make every day the first so I never get too cocky about my sobriety) mc, cracker...are a dream come true for skinheads. Remember this unwritten handshake we've just handshook because you've read what I wrote...these are skinhead words. I would gather or imagine there aren't many white supremacists reading a book created by a

lesbian who has multi-racial relationships. This is why I

fear not the neo Nazi finding out the fact that I just

called them out. I also give permission to use any hateful

term you'd like for some idiot who supports genocide

and some maniac with an unusual mustache, who was

really angry. REALLY angry...perhaps his mother

molesting him regularly helped lead him toward

vegetarian painting. He had no problem killing droves of

people in mass quantities...but nary the thought of

eating meat. True story.


Who made up cock block? Isn't that relatively new? How

about cunt rag? How positively delightful is that term?

And which genius started calling his buddies douche

bag? Who the hell invented this delicious item of hygiene? The word douche, I realize, means shower in French. I don't think they intended for it to mean something you shove up your vagina and clean it out. Was there a Mr. Tampon? I sure am sorry I missed out on the sanitary napkin contraption that had belted a rag, uncomfortably on your bottom. I'm sure girls with their period during the time of the ladies jockstrap, asked their closest friends every 18 seconds, while turning your back to them, "Is there anything on the back of my skirt, pants, short, collates?" in the event that some leakage could have taken place. Sorry boys, you'll have to deal with at least a couple of vaginal hygiene comments. Think of it as an education. And for all the grown boys who feel absolutely nothing about standing in a long line, while his friend approaches him and begins to converse, holding the super plus (make sure you get the orange box!) tampons, GOOD FOR YOU! And rock on for the girls who are smart enough to buy their own condoms.

Why is forensic science so wildly televised when we're teaching psychopaths how to commit the perfect crime? I watch them relentlessly. I'm pretty sure I could pull off serial killing. Not that I would, so calm your underpants.

Why in the hell would you wrap lambskin around your penis and why would a woman allow that into her lady friend. Not only do they smell like rotten milk but they're porous as well. People....it's the skin of a lamb you're using around your genitals. Would you slap a steak on your member to enhance this magical

moment?

Yo-yo?

Ottoman? Some poor slob named Otto who followed his

friend around and waited for him to sit? Make the

experience a little more comfortable?

My father once proceeded to eat half of a shellacked

bagel because he just assumed it was terribly stale...but

he was starving. I don't know if none of us had the heart

to tell him or if we thought in some way...it maybe did

taste like stale bagel.

Why on earth would I eat a fried squirrel with a spike

driven through its head coming out of its ass? Why am I

able to tell you frogs legs taste like fishy chicken as does

alligator. Rattlesnake is delicious. And how do people fry

jellybeans without melting them. I'm pretty curious

about the fried ball of ice cream as well. How fat would

you like to become before you order anything like a fried

Twinkie, fried snickers, fried dough....well, I'll tell you

what all of that tastes like. They say you get fat when

you're happy. Well, I must have been downright jovial!

The fact that they made Count Dracula a character on

Sesame Street as a counter is brilliant! How's that for

disarming the children and their fear of monsters? "See, honey?! Dracula doesn't mutilate people! He counts!"

Where do names like Shaqueesha come from? And, again, I'm not meaning to offend...I truly want to know where Sharmarlaquain came from? I watch Maury on my days off. I'm fascinated by someone being a trillion percent sure, and this man sure "Is not the father!" And continues to test 5 other men she's all a trillion percent sure all 5 of them know he's the father. None of them, of course, are the father, which means that girl slept with at least 6 men in one month...and I haven't so much as touched a boob, unless it an accidental graze, in two years...maybe more.

Parents, you are smothering the shit out of your kids. I made it a hobby of skinning my knees and look at me now? Oh Jesus, maybe it was the knee skinning that turned me into a wino. Ok....bring the out in a bulletproof vest and a catcher's mask...and oversized chin guards that ride clear up the thigh. We don't need any more pissies than we already have. I'm gonna call science on this one.

I'd like to know why EVERY SINGLE TIME...I see someone from my past, I ask them how their mother is and not only is their mother dead but, I attended the funeral.

I have the attention span of a goldfish. This is why this book makes no sense.

I'm addicted to my electric cigarette. Has it helped me slow down on regular cigarettes? Bet your bippy. Yet, if I set my electric cigarette down or forgot to pack an extra for my day, I absolutely become agitated beyond comprehension.

Why were Cheng and Eng (the first famous conjoined twins aka Siamese Twins...is that the correct terminology? Are they dual heads? Unattached maybe? Difficult to masturbate or use a toilet.) anyhoo...why did Cheng and Eng find wives and I can't? How can you make love to your wife with your brother hanging off the side of you? Can you blindfold him? Will he ejaculate? Did the wives essentially want a built in orgy....I GOT IT....they were secretly lesbian lovers in a time where being gay was less acceptable than being a circus sideshow. So they plotted to bring a bouquet of dandelions to the left half so the right one can smile. When they proposed, did they get on their knees? This is quickly spinning out of control. Now I seem like connected bigot. Seriously though....did they have one set of sex organs and one rectum or did everything in the pant level remain as one? If it was one, based on two combined, does that make them really well endowed?

Dr. Sigmund Freud had a cocaine habit that resembled Tony Montana and yet, we still see is teachings as poignant. Now, to all of my friends who have used coke, you know that the more you shell out, the better your idea gets about why things are the way they are. Basically, he was a deranged cokehead who never slept and I would imagine only seldom ate. Tell me how you feel after being up 24 hours straight...not to mention 36, 72 etc,. Because I'll tell you, I start to identify with Jack Torrance (if you don't know this reference, I recommend you not only look it up, but watch it.

If I had a red Corvette, I would clearly only play that song. I long to not only be that closet dweeb. (Yes, I said dweeb...which really makes me a dweeb...because who says dweeb anymore?) but, a real live one as well!

How did it go from Billiards to Pool? Seems to me that

pool already had its hooks into the swimming apparatus.

Is the big difference the net ball holder (three words

you'd very seldom say in a lifetime) as opposed to the

ball rolling slot (again...to each his own. I won't knock it

till I try it)

How about football vs. soccer? Was it us that stole the

football thing and rearranged it?

How did they get away with making a show like "All in

the Family" without causing major race wars? Not to

mention constantly calling his wife dingbat. Now, if Edith

didn't have the battered wife posture while she walked,

I'll eat my hat.

Why do we say, "I'll eat my hat!"? Which fella on the strip said, "If you have $10 in your pocket, I'll eat my hat?" Has anyone actually ever lost that bet?

Do we not realize when we call someone a son of a bitch we're not offending them, rather their mother. Which yes, could cause a scuffle. It's still not about you. Unless of course they mean your mother was a female dog, in which case make you a puppy, in which case would make you sub-human. Maybe they're dying to pet you and this was all they could think of.

How about Bastard? How did a term used to insult children born out of wedlock (another twisted, right wing, maniacal sociopaths invention) become something we use freely. I mean, if I feel bad for a person, my sentence will always start, "this poor bastard....."

FUCK: Fornication under Church and King....its origin did indeed mean sex. When did it become a vocalized pause or an adjective?

Why would you talk horribly about someone in a foreign language when upon you can't be totally sure...they're not fluent in your native language too, genius?

Julia Roberts...I mean with all of my might...I adore you and think you're an amazing actor...but I have to address the elephant in the room. Pretty Woman was about a whore moving in with a John. We didn't see the day before Gere pulled up in the sports car when Cinder-fuckin-rella was sucking some 70 year old, unwashed ass. Hhookkkeeeerrrr.....she was a prostitute!

Um.....

Amaaaaaaaazziinnnggg Grraaccceeee....how su-weet the-uh ssooouunnndddd....thaAaat ssavveeedddd aaaa WRETCH?! A little extreme, no? That's the best word that could have been used? I mean, who was this author looking at right at the moment that the word Wretch came to mind?

Whoever came up with elephant in the room was very clever.

If you're a bigot in any way, it would behoove you to not become a counselor. Or at least keep it in your shirt until you get home. You can't pray the gay away, you can't Brillo the color of someone's skin unless, of course, you're Michael Jackson in which case you see where that'll take you. Noseless in a pine box. Doesn't seem worth it. I mean, if you're gonna go, better to go with a nose I say!

I would stand in the doorway of the living room either playing with a yo-yo, even though I admit, I have no idea why it's a yo-yo, a hula hoop...hand flipping it onto the floor so it was go forward for a bit and then speed race back to you or, piece du resistance ...kabangers. Broken handle dangerous titanium alloy danger orbs attached to a shoelace. Get a good momentum and then *BAM*. I believe this might have been the early stages of things like cutting or burning. Only if you want to risk your life, will you clack clack clack clack BAM right off the forearm. Had we all gone to school looking like maybe we had track marks? Now they made the shoe lace, plastic so they cannot give you a compound fracture in your forearm. My point is...I did three of the most annoying, distracting things you could ever do in life, in that room where everyone was watching Laverne and

Shirley and I never once got yelled at. My parents are

AWESOME!!


If you drink eggnog too fast, it will give you a stomach

ache. My mother was right.


In the event you do get said belly ache, put a tablespoon

of baking soda in half a glass of lukewarm water. It's

disgusting, so do it fast. The nausea will POOF disappear.


Yes, an anxiety attack does feel like a heart attack.

Jodie Foster was the suntan advertisement with the puppy pulling down the baby's diaper, only to reveal a bright white ass on a dark brown tan. These day it's 37 million SPF before the child even sits down on a chair in the living room that has a ray of sun in the center of the rug.

I slipped on an itchy ball during softball practice....and got a compound fracture in my forearm. One way or another I was going to succeed in getting lots of attention. Did I get a hot pink cast? Bet your ass I did. Also landed on the same boy during spin the bottle 3 times in a row and we were supposed to go in the closet, I rigged a sexy black light that is generally about 5 billion degrees Celsius, so extra safe exposed on plain wood right underneath the exposed asbestos insulation.

Better believe I'm expecting mesothelioma any day

now! Anyways, in the closet for my 7 minutes in heaven

with the boy I really liked and cracked him in the head

with my concrete arm. He still asked me out after having

a boys meeting in the bathroom. I didn't realize they had

board meetings about such a decision. So, he called my

best friend while she was away seeing family that he's

breaking up with her and asking me out. What a shitty

friend I was to allow that. Eh...I was 12.


There's a saying that reads, "Physician heal thyself" in

my case it's,"clinician heal thyself." I find it amazing that

I am able to sincerely give sound advice to people in

need. Let's face it, if you're sitting across from me, you

need some help. I love my job. It brings me peace. It challenges me. It allows me to watch people who have been out down their whole life, succeed. Of course, it has its rough patches and I have to get a hold of my heart and realize not everyone can be helped. I pride myself on a decent turnaround. I truly believe that it is because I love what I do.

Advice from my grandmother, who was my absolute, best friend in life....who I admit, I am still basically in denial about her passing, although my brain registers it, my heart would rather believe she's on vacation. She had many lovely tidbits of knowledge...say, for instance, "if a lezzy wants to take you on a vacation to Florida, then take the vacation. Who cares if she's a lezzie. Just don't let her in when you're taking a bath. Unless you want her in there. It's up to you." My grandmother was the first to accept and ream my family members about my coming out. She never even flinched, "so what if she's a lezzy, she's still Sarah! What's wrong with you?!" Anyway, that's obviously not the advice I initially set out with, however if the situation fits, lock the bathroom door. My grandmother said 2 things that we always repeat in our family. First is: Always have your own buck. Don't ever depend on any bastard to take care of you, cause you never know when they'll be gone. And B: (yes, I realize I do say "first" for my first thought and "B' for my second. It's my prerogative) you spend 8 or more hours a day at where you woyk (which is work in grandma slang) if you hate your job, leave it. You'll be miserable all the time. Find a job that you love...and you'll always be happy!" My grandmother used to take 3 buses to go to her risky job in a dry cleaner, before air conditioning was affordable enough. So she sat over unbearable steam in 100 degree heat while her and the girls would drink warm beer. So if you have an old piece of clothing whose pant press is off to the hard left, my grandmother and her girls got a hold of it. Then, she would take about 2 more buses to go to her job at the cafeteria of a college. I'm not sure if she continued the beer at that job...I'm thinking no. Now, as uncomfortable as both of these jobs seem, she made the best of it. She worked with her friends, who I spent the better portion of my young life with, which is why I know how to smuggle out a plastic bag full of silverware and half of the all you can eat salad bar. I'm pretty sure we walked out of restaurant one night with about 14lbs of shrimp,

2 carafes, a salt and pepper shaker and all of the cloth napkins they could spare. We had so much shrimp salad; there were not just enough napkins to wipe the extra amount of salt and pepper. Good thing we had those carafes full of water mixed with the lemon that came extra with tea. No one at the table was drinking tea so I was amazed at the 15 extra lemon dishes they were bringing us. We never saw the silverware again. Black market perhaps. Anyway...I digress, even if we both have no idea what the original idea is after I've given my family away as Grand Theft Restaurant. And since I have the ability to touch and run my finger up a screen to find out where we were and you may be turning a page, it would ruin my concentration to do that so, just keep up!)I'll get us back...what I was saying is, it's amazing the advice I'm able to give to people on the most obvious

issues, that I positively refuse to follow myself. Let's say,

for instance, someone you call a friend has at least on 2

occasions, possibly more but the brain can have a funny

way of deleting shitty goods into the archive section,

said to you, "I really don't give a shit what you think!"

On, say, matters of the heart. If you happen to be upset

about something or, if you tell that same friend you

need to talk about something and they basically tell you

they'll see if they have an opening next week. That's a

beauty I've gotten from not one but TWO friends.

Naturally....what would my advice be? What would

YOUR advice be? Simple, right? If that person says things

like that to you, they're obviously not your friend, right?

The last thing in the world you need are negative

people. A true friend would find a minute to help you

through a tough situation. Do you think this is the advice

I keep? Maybe. Do you think it took me years to

accomplish? Bet your sweet ass it did. If a client talks to

me about not having sex with their spouse for well over

a year, close to two, am I going to say, "Have you tried

new things? Have you spoken to them about why?

Maybe have that person come in and sit down with us

and we'll try to figure out why this is happening?" But

might I be thinking, "if they haven't had sex with you in

over a year...A: they're repulsed by you or you are

repulsed by them and second: if they say nothing about

it and don't seem to care, more than likely, they're

screwing someone else. If a client comes in and wonders

why they're ex still can't be friends anymore after you

dumped them clear in the middle of knowing they are

desperately in love with you, I might say something fun

like, "well, maybe they're having a tough time separating

from you, romantically, right now. Maybe, give them some space and time to heal. Get used to the idea that that dimension of your relationship no longer exists." I might be thinking, "you narcissistic asshole. You don't get to have it both ways. How dare you even pretend to think that's acceptable. You know what...stay away from them and let them heal. All you're doing is throwing a heaping cup of salt on the carved out part of their chest where I vital muscle once lived!" My mind was opened and educated by my therapist when I said, "oh, I just want her to be happy." and she said, "Oh, that's bullshit. This woman has clearly made her choice to move on with someone else. Forget this "wishing her well" stuff. She doesn't deserve it or you." Another reason I want to marry her. If someone makes you second, you're an asshole for making them first. I've seen so many of my friends and family think that this stupid piece of paper keeps you bound to someone you clearly hate. I know there are a variety of other reasons. Maybe you're a stay at home mom/dad and rely on the income, which is where grandma's advice can be utilized. Maybe it's a domestic violence issue, which cannot be found funny in any capacity. I which case battered wife/ husband (yes, husbands can also be victims. If you don't believe me, check out about 80% of the crime shows on television....lots of angry women. A level of gentle needs to come out of you that's calmer than with a newborn because with any luck, you will be able to give this person the option of feeling reborn. My very favorite excuse is.....say it with me now....for the sake of the kids. Unbearable. Are you really under the impression that kids don't pick up on every little bit of ignorance, tension from screaming, tension from silence, the necessity they feel to talk their head off as a means to keep the room light? One of my best friends, a best friend who supports and protects me by being absolutely real all the time. This woman stands by her friends with such ferocity, she should teach a class on it. Has 3 sons all at very impressionable ages....figuring like 6, 10 and 14....around those ages. Realized her relationship with her husband was so toxic, that they would, in fact, be BETTER parents, if they did it separately. Took the courageous, actually, had balls of steel leaving her very co-dependent husband with a very short fuse and did this with her head held high. Raises these three boys while working a full time, very difficult job, going to school to further her career and teaches in her field as well....does she get home and drop on the bed? She sure doesn't. She makes sure her boys are well fed, well supported with things like activities, homework, sports etc. and most importantly, those 3 boys know why mommy is doing what she's doing to give them a better life. And even mmooorrrreeeee important than that, she prevents them from living in a volatile situation because she loves them more than air and will do anything to show them that you follow your heart and never settle for less. This is the kind of woman who will remember at midnight that she wasn't able to text you back during the day due to her superhuman life. She'll text you to tell you she loves you and that she almost broke her toe in getting to that phone in Olympic fashion when she realized she had forgotten. Funny thing is this friend and I got off to a very rocky start. I'm surprised a conversation with her even took place after our first meeting but, for some reason, I felt like she could handle the criticism like an adult and maybe throw something back at me. From that conversation on....Diana, you rank up there with the goods. You are a marine in my world. Anyone who has a friend, who is half the woman I see in her, is the luckiest person on earth. I refuse to give any further information, because I will not let anyone steal her....I'm greedy.

As a matter of fact, I'd have to say the 2 friends I have that are ferociously loyal are both Hispanic....I highly recommend seeking those out. Second friend has been an absolute lion when it comes to standing next to me has been doing that since we're 14. Christina, you also deserve a loud WOW!! Another woman who was strong enough to leave a toxic relationship AND managed to salvage a civilized friendship with her ex. She has always and will never settle than less than who and what she deserves.

And of course...there's My Jenn. Amazingly 2 of these women have been my best friends for 23 years. When you can start saying that, you're old. Nobody believes you befriended one another as a zygote. In closing while again, trying to figure out where this all started...got it....don't settle for anything or anyone less than you deserve. As a matter of fact, bullshit! Don't settle until what you deserve is so far surpassed, you're positive God...or your higher power....wrapped this person up in recycled paper towels used from curing the demons inside...and sent that angel right to you. Priority. That person could be right in front of you and you're just not paying attention. It happens.

Positively no one, except maybe the most rigid dentist, brushes their teeth in circles. And we're told to use soft bristle toothbrushes and buy toothpaste for sensitive teeth. Well, I go home and slop up my rock solid bristles that could remove paint, with "please whiten the shit out of my teeth" even if it sends shock waves up into your face.

That being said....it is not normal for anyone to bite down on an ice pop with their 2 front teeth, is just unnatural and sadistic. It will ruin my whole day if I'm with someone who does that. As a matter of fact, I have awful chills right now just thinking about it. Now, every goddamn person I know is going to chomp down. Even if it hurts them, just to bust my balls.

You really never realize how much you love and miss your parents, until they've gone away.  My mother recently went to see her sister, my aunt in case you couldn't put that together. Usually, I drove my mother there and picked her up, no snap. Well.....dad did it. Dad answers his phone on speaker. I gave him specific instructions on where and how to get her. Since I am in school 2 blocks away, I went to meet her and wait. She was going to need to be picked up at around 1:00 so naturally she tells him to be there at noon. Now, for whatever reason, my father who used to drive a Daily News truck all over Manhattan, is completely perplexed on how he could take one street that will take him straight to the corner of 33rd and 8th. "Howd'ja get there. You can't believe the traffic. Is there a taxi stand there....because the traffic unreal, now is she getting off at 7th, because the cars are just piled up on each other." Dad, is there any traffic? Gee whiz. Anyway, go through Bayonne, NJ and take the Holland Tunnel, it literally leaves you right at that one Hudson which turns into 8th" "Absolutely not! Do you have any idea what the lines to that thing looks like a parking lot with all of those cars?" Well, dad, you're asking me for directions. This is the way I always go." Well, what about if I just go through the tunnel?" Did I not just say go through the tunnel?!" "Christ's sake, the tunnel that takes you to the West Side Highway!" "Again, I have no idea how to get anywhere aside from the route I've been driving for almost 20 years. I always feel like if I take one of those NYC tunnels, that you have to go through from New York to New York, something will go horribly wrong." "What could wrong!? You think it would be an overload of traffic? Boy that traffic can get pretty ugly. (Damn traffic again) I have to pick mommy up at 12. (As I giggled with guilt that was not gonna happen) what time should I leave the house? Like 4 am.....say it with me now.....because there's gonna be traffic. Isn't the President in town? They shut down all the streets. Probably why it's so backed up." Dad, I'm standing here on the corner you are supposed to get to and there are most certainly cars. I highly doubt that a woman driving a Big Bird colored VW bug is a member of the secret service....unless, of course, she's a decoy. I which case, I am brilliant at cracking conspiracy plans.

## Blackouts and Agoraphobia

2 years ago I was diagnosed agoraphobic. For those of you, who don't know what that mean, lift up the rock you're under and I'll tell you....

It means that you have a terrible, horrendous fear of leaving your comfort zone. In my case, it was my bedroom. The anxiety that washes over you while even considering leaving this place causes debilitating anxiety. Usually you'll find some reason to not go anywhere. I had run out of options of excuses I would make in order to crawl back in bed and let out a sigh of relief. Although still the terror is very real and constantly looming over you that at some point you will have to show your face or you will lose your friends and your family will be perpetually angry with you but terrified that you're also going to die. Now the anxiety kicks in about canceling with that friend because you ruined their night...and then they find another friend to go with and you'll see their pictures on some social media nightmare and feel upset because they look like they're having a good time and you wished you had gone. The next time you are invited you decide you have to go so the terror is washing over you. You feel like you're choking to death in the shower. Getting dressed is a nightmare because you're completely out of shape from doing nothing but lay around. Nothing fits right, so you sit on the edge of your bed panting. Wondering what you can say in order to cancel. You know you can't, so you throw on whatever fits and out the door you go...horrified every step of the way. So what's driving you? In my case, I knew it was a little baggie of coke and a bottle of tequila. The beer is only there as an accessory. As long as I have drugs and alcohol in me I know the night will be great! Now I'm outside the bar/club/Moose lodge...ridiculously early. There are 4 people in the bar and the band is just taking their equipment off the truck. Before I even take my coat off, I order 3 shots of Patron back to back. Then I'll get my prop beer and wait for the person who's packing snow. (Snow=coke...to those people under the rock) eh, I would get loaded and inevitably make an asshole out of myself. Needless to say, the next day when woke up at 3 because I had been doing the coke until 7 in the morning. I would look at my phone and see these elaborately written nonsense texts to just about anyone on my phone. In which case, I would then heighten my agoraphobia.

Today, I am the project coordinator of a brand new business....which entails me often having to stand in front of a classroom of up to 45 people. So....that doctor can shove his agoraphobia up his ass....and you can pause if I ask you if I look fat and say "fine" after I've spent 2 hours getting ready. Fact is my brain is sexy. I'd choose that any day of the week!

Blackouts:

This...my friends...is the NUMBER ONE reason I love being sober. What I learned was the alcohol wasn't doing a thing to help my anxiety...it only made it severely worse. It didn't help me sleep, it just kept me in a REM like state where I never really knew what was real and what wasn't. Still, to this day...I really have no clue about a lot of things. I've worked through just letting it go and getting on with my life with as much of a level of forgiveness as I can.

Generally, when your friend who has about as much rhythm as your front lawn is standing with the lead singer of the band screaming, "....WITH A REBEL YELL...SHE CRIED MO MO MO OH OH..." She's not awake. She is having a blackout. When your schoolteacher friend is standing on the bar dancing to, "I'm walking on sunshine" which she oddly played repeatedly throughout the night and does actually show her tits when that request was yelled at her by some dumpy 60 something year old man, with Viagra in his pocket.....she's probably right in the throes of a blackout. If your very married friend just walked into the men's room with the best man...and that door remains locked as the line forms to about 45 very peepee riddled men...she'd better either be in a blackout or learn how to just know when to say you're having a blackout when suitable. If your bartender friend (cough cough...that would be this asshole) is going shot for shot with a biker gang post funeral for one of their brothers...she's definitely mentally unconscious. When in these situations...do not stop to think...just jump and remove her. If you have to make a deal with one of your friends to not "do too many shots tonight!" Leave her home. Blackout victims i.e.: the innocent bystander and or collateral damage...yes, who you're looking at by midnight is not your friend. Your friend went home to bed 2 hours ago. She just left her body behind for you to deal with. Chances are they'll either start screaming crying for no reason whatsoever. You'll be floored and crazed at what the hell just happened. You're all set to start swinging because your fab friend over here is a mess of snot (quirp...that's my gag reflex...snot or any derivative herein is an absolute no no in my world) tears, shit coming out of her mouth. Her hair is soaked. Have no idea why her hair is soaked but, it is indeed soaked. You're trying to ask her what the hell happened while the bouncer is trying to escort both of you out. You'll then spend the entire night listening to her sob about how sad she was when her Uncle Jack died when she was only 10 but she rreealllyyyy lloooovveedddd hiimmmm.....so, for that, you've just left a pretty good time talking to a pretty decent digit swap because Red Rain was Uncle Jack's favorite song and it came on the jukebox...compliments of?!?! You got it...slopp-o in your front seat. She'll get progressively worse the more you try to reason with her that "Uncle Jack will always be with you *yawn*". You see that potential first date walk outside with someone else, you're furious, you start up the car...WHICH YOU ALSO SHOULD NOT BE DOING...as a drunk, I crashed my cars at least 5 times...one time I got out to see the wreckage and proceeded to slide backwards down into a muddy ravine about 25 feet. Guess what? The brilliant cop who helped me out of the swamp...LET ME GOOOO! Anyway...off course, as usual...you'll drive Jack's niece home. Wake her half dead ass up to get the fuck out of your car. She'll wake up and smile with her wet hair stuck in her mouth (quirp...gag reflex). She'll act like she's endearingly going to touch your face but she's so hammered, she basically slaps you. She might tell you she secretly falling in love with you...which is just transference because you were the hero that night. You'll get her into bed, take off the horrendously difficult boots she's wearing, pat her on her head, hope for the best and head home. The next morning you'll get a text on how hilarious last night was...because why?!...that's right...she was asleep. You're an awesome friend for caring, for getting her home safely, for sacrificing your good time because of fucking Jack...yes, the blackout was real. Make your life a lot easier and do a very difficult thing. Tell your friend she needs help and follow through on an ultimatum. Ask for help yourself....we recovery folks are everywhere! And I'm not some rah rah cheerleader for recovery...I just know that if I didn't die and I'm sitting here sharing

my story with you...better believe I can pay that forward

every single time I'm asked.

**This is the chapter I call...chapter**

I live in New York. I've basically lived in NY my whole life

because even when I found myself someplace else, NY

was always home to me. For those of you who don't

understand New York City, it is broken down into 5

boroughs. New York City (obviously), Brooklyn, Queens,

Boogie Down Bronx and Staten Island. I'm a Staten

Islander. Was formerly famous for the largest garbage

dump in the world. That is a myth. Staten Island is one of

the prettiest, close knit communities you'll ever

encounter. You get the florally, park, old men playing softball kinda town with the hustle and a bustle (yes, I said and a bustle...it's my book. I can do anything I want) of NYC. Now, most true New Yorkers forget to even acknowledge the beauty of the city because we're cattle driving to and from work. We're big fans of tourists doing something clever like moo-ing or goofily saying, "what is this a cattle drive?! Is this a cattle drive?! Mmoooooooo...." Real clever, dingbat. In case you haven't noticed the sea of tired eyes and briefcases snarling quietly at you, I recommend you keep your screaming children from chasing after each other whipping each other with scarves while we become collateral damage. That's the thought of a New Yawka. I'm guessing anyone from a foreign country wouldn't be ok with us swarmed in front of their office standing 24 feet away from their spouse in order to take her picture while everyone waits for the click of the camera. I've seen whole traffic jams that started with a girl giving the hard thumbs up in front of George Washington. It wasn't pretty.

In any event...at this point of writing the book, I'm 37. I have never been to or even seen the Empire State Building, I went to the Statue of Liberty once when I was a teenager. I don't think I've ever been to Central Park..I got stoned a lot in parks. Chances are pretty good I was in Central Park. I've never skated at Rockefeller Center. I promised myself if never go see that damn tree until I'm with someone whose hand I wanna hold. Yeah...good luck with that, Schmitty! New York, at any given time, obviously has a plethora of any single nationality at once. See, what happened to me recently (this is because even though I get aggravated with behavior of the mooing and whatnot, I'm still very polite, there was a man who appeared very agitated asking me a question. I couldn't understand the beginning of the sentence. All I heard was something that sounded like "raunch". I kept tilting my head like a dog you keep asking, "you wanna go OUT?! Wanna go for a WALK?! Wanna go for a WALK!". My eyebrows were scrunched together because clearly if I lower my eyebrows, I would be able to understand better. Now, every time I looked confused or, just had my mouth open (also another way to understand someone) he would become more agitated and eventually was just flat it screaming, "MUMBLE MUMBLE MUMBLE WONG SHEV RETCH....RUNCH?!" Holy shit, I'm thinking. Now, I'm surrounded by no less than 100 people and not a single one could see the desperation in my eyes. Not one of those people even turned to throw me a life preserver. I continued to be polite and for some reason I thought shouting and pointing at my ear would help him to understand that I did not speak his language. Well, he persevered so I figured I must too. Well, finally he began to make a movement like he was bringing a utensil up to his mouth. And it dawned on me, "HE WANTS TO KNOW WHERE TO GET LUNCH?!" Which is an absurd thing to ask when there are 5 places to get food in the terminal alone and outside of the ferry, there is just about every kind of eatery you'd like within one block. Now I'm stuck with the next part of this conversation. Now he and I are just full on shouting at each other. People who couldn't hear the words but, rather the tones, thought we were fighting pretty viciously. And yet still.....not a helping hand in sight. Now, this snippet is not made to insult anyone so please read on and you'll see my reason for this. Instead of accepting my response of THERE ARE MANY KINDS OF RESTAURANTS IN THE AREA!!! While rapidly mimicking a spoon coming up to my mouth and twirling my finger in the air because those two things are sign language for "there are many different eateries in the area." Sooner or later I was either going to twirl my fingers like I'm rolling spaghetti to mean Italian food, take two pens out of my bag and create chopsticks, hold my hands up to my face in a pinch motion like I'm eating a sandwich for a deli, I don't know what the hell to do with Indian food...from what I believe it's generally with your fingers (you'll notice I never search anything on the internet because I clearly feel like my way is a lot more fun) you can't explain Irish food and I refuse to look like

I'm holding a beer up to my face because that's far too stereotypical. German food I'd only have some luck pointing to his peepee. Well, maybe not HIS peepee but a peepee nonetheless. (This reference is made because I'm thinking of various schnitzel type food items. Hence, the shape of a peepee) If he's Vegan, he's shit it of luck and if he wanted French food I would surely feel like I needed to do something cliche like wear a beret. I refuse to do any of those things. So here I stand, seemingly arguing with this man. Now, from what I understand...and by all means, correct me if I'm wrong, Asian languages are a tone language?  So I'm guessing on occasion when most of us enter an Asian restaurant and they all sound like they're going to kill each other is basically just part of the emphasis. The difference is, you see, this individual was just flat out pissed off at me.

Now we're getting to, "RUNCH RUNCH YOU

KNOW....RUNCH!" "Yes, I get you. YOOOUUUUU

WWAAANNNTTTTT LLUUNNCCCHHHH (he can hear me

if I scream louder, clearly) There are

MMMAAANNNYYYYYY DIIIIFFFFF-a-RREEEENNNTTTT

PLLLAACCEEEESSSSS TO EEEAAATTTTT (imaginary fork

up to face imaginary fork up to face imaginary fork up to

face)IN TTHHIIISSSSS AARREEEEAAAAA (twirling my

finger in the air twirling my finger in the air twirling my

finger in the air)! Now finally this very Staten Island, gum

snappin' lotsa hair and probably always well manicured,

very long fingernails, steps up to the plate. I'm breathing

a sigh of relief before she  yell out, "what'd a hell are you

talkin'about?! Dere's (Staten Island guido for "there's") a

Chinese rest-or-rant outside...Ooouuuutttt

Ssiiiiiddeeeee!" Now she's doing the little finger walk

imitation on the palm of her hand because that is also universal language for, um, walk. Now, in this small paragraph, I have imitated and could very well may have insulted two groups of people but the point of this is, first of all, not everyone in Staten Island talks like a Jersey Shore (TV show for any of you reading this book past 2015) character and not every Asian person says the ridiculous imitations some people are dumb enough to do. Nothing is sexier than going out to dinner with some ass who will look at the waiter and say, "oh, I have a pawk fly lice, uh shlimp with a robster sauce." Because every one of us has an asshole acquaintance in our life that will think it's hilarious when not only is it wildly offensive but embarrassing. Now, the man walks away clearly aggravated and I feel defeated because I couldn't shout where I thought was a nice place for him to eat so that he wouldn't struggle terribly with the menu and wind up in another screaming match. In the end, after his departure, this dimwit with the clicking nails, chewing him 80 mph smelling like she took a dip what smelled like women's Obsession, looks at me and says....yes she sure does, "this izzzz fockin' AmeriCa...learn how to speak fockin' Eng-a-lesh *pop pop pop of the gum in between her two front teeth* and then the bomb drops...."fuckin' gooks should go back to where the fock he came from.....ya know?! *snap snap snap the gum* fuckin' gook!" I froze...I froze like Frosty without his magic hat. I froze because apparently her peripheral and non peripheral is on the fritz. We were surrounded by so many people who could have and should have been offended. Including myself. Suddenly, of course, all eyes were on me and I'm the type of person who turns scarlet when I'm embarrassed and I embarrass easily. If I have the hiccups I get embarrassed. For whatever reason I felt like I was utterly responsible...and yet dingbat continued on her rave about, "dey take ova fockin' everyting, ya know?! Fokin' egg roll moths focka!" Now....egg roll was the last straw but I wanted to make sure I handled this with dignity and not turn into her, which generally happens when I get angry. Not her pretty terminology but the accent....it's killer when I'm angry. So I stood there for an instant and thought, "you know what fuckin' gets me?! (Because I wanted her to believe I was on her side) she's snapping, cracking and popping her gun with half a smirk on my face and said....I'd love to see you trapped in China and even have a whack at asking someone where you could get lunch. Even better, wouldn't it be cool if you were in an Asian owned establishment and could really understand what incredibly offensive things they were saying about you?!" She stared at me disgustedly. Blank but with utter disgust although something tells me she has that look on her face until she gets 19 kamikaze shots in her and makes out with as many hard hair boys as she could. "I know if I wound up in, lets say China, and was starving to death, no level of air spooning or screaming of the word "LUNCH" would get me anything but a snobby bitch cursing me out in a language I'll never understand." Here's what we forget....not every non-English speaking person you come across, is not an American Citizen. Do I believe that if you live here, you should speak English? Positively. However, we are one of those travel destinations people only dream of. So, if this Asian man even so much as knew the word lunch but had a problem with the L....do me a favor, approach

a Spanish speaking person and ask them for chile relleno

and see how you fair. As a matter of fact, skip on over to

a French citizen and tell him that you'd love a ham

sandwich on toasted rye with mayo without using a

translation dictionary. You see, even though,yes...it is

frustrating to have to bob and weave through folks who

think nothing of stopping competely short to take a

picture of a wreath on a building on a bank. Fascinating

stuff. But let us not forget that it is not an easy vacation

destination if you don't speak a lick of English....but they

try. They have more balls than the rest of us. Particularly

in difficult languages like, Chinese, Japanese ( and if

you're saying 'dirty knees...look at these!', you're not

alone, because I most assuredly did it.) Russian,

Icelandic, even a very thick Irish brogue, I would freeze

up behind who I was traveling with and pray to God they'll be able to successfully tell us where to find a ladies room. I admire some of these tourists for throwing caution to the wind and trying their hardest to ask for help. It's more the international tourists who speak English perfectly but have the common sense of a nickel. I know these people work and should have a tiny bit of consideration for those of us carrying attaché cases sporting a hard scowl on her faces. If you decide to take the beautiful, scenic ride to look at the magnificent Statue of Liberty. Not to to mention the picturesque skyline during sunset. Maybe, please try not to hit these tourist attractions during rush hour ie:7am until 6:00pn at the very least. And for the love of God, stop with the mooing. It resembles a cattle drive because it is a gaggle of people who have been out somewhere 8 to 16 hours at a job they could very well hate. I'm fortunate...I love my job but, I still wanna get home by 7pm after leaving the house by 6am. If it happens to be rush hour home....I recommend that you duct tape the mouth and body of your very loud shriller of a child. Few things on earth are more aggravating than being forced into a game of peekaboo with an incessant giggler. And don't make us feel bad by singing, "now now, Madison, leave the nice lady alone. She doesn't seem to want to play." Great, so make me look like the ogre so your child gets that embarrassed look on their face which then turns into a spoiled brat cry. If you're rocking your 10 year old to console them, you're twisted and they're spoiled. Unless that child has a compound fracture, you shouldn't even be considering the , "ookkkkkk oookkkkkk, sssh ssh ssh sssh....ookkkkkk ookkkkkk.....maybe somebody else wants to play...sshhheeee sssshhhh...." Hey dickhead, here's an idea ....why don't you play an hour long game of peekaboo with your twisted pre adolescent. You can even let them throw on your fancy styrofoam Statue of Liberty halo that you look so non-touristy in. It would be like me wearing a red and white horizontal striped fitted shirt, black stretch pants and a black beret through France....while you're trying to battle peekaboo the whole way home. I would understand that Mon Dieu means "My God." I would know if you called me a pig. I would know if you wanted a ham and cheese sandwich. So, should I ever visit France and I'm eating ham and Swiss on bread (I can't be specific. I can only say bread...so I have to say "bread" and hope for the best) in a church, don't call me a pig. These are the only things I know how to say. Unless you feel it necessary to call me pig, in which case I would hear only the word "pig" and not understand the rest of the sentence anyway so I could either be offended or wonder if you're telling me that you knew the pig whose ham I'm currently eating.

However, my real point is this. Maybe you'll approach me and say something like, "you will tell how to get a cheese a burger? And I'll admittedly know you're a tourist but what you won't know about me is how much I admire you coming to a strange country doing your best to communicate in my language. This is why I will stand in front of an Asian man screaming RUNCH at me and dammit...I'm gonna do my best to figure out what kinda RUNCH he wants. It's guidette Toni that I will have no patience for yelling at my new hungry friend. First because her first language is English and yet she still speaks it terribly. Any American leading a tour group, do me a favor....tell these folks that I'm proud of them for taking the risk of never being able to get a decent meal because no one will know what kind of RUNCH they really want. And don't think for one second, I wasn't one of those close minded assholes that was just as quick to almost walk them clear into a Chinese restaurant....because who doesn't fly thousands of miles to plant themselves down in front of a meal they can have at home every damn day of their lives.

God Bless the tourist, who has no clue what they're walking into, yet takes the chance anyway. I know my ass couldn't get off a flight to Japan and yell anything at all but Hibachi. That, once again, would lead me into dickhead land.

So to the tourists who visit our fine country...including our amazing city, I congratulate you for carrying your little translation dictionary and giving it a shot. Please, If at all possible, try to make your overly photographed Statue of Liberty shots anywhere from 10:30 am to 2 pm and if that's not possible....I recommend you don't moo. Some of the smartest people in the world are on that boat. The mooing only makes them feel frustrated and they will direct you to the nearest hotdog vendor and yell Bon appetit!

**And now for some sound advice and how I really think...chapter**

Anger drives us. Sometimes it makes us succeed because we're ready to take on the fight. More times, however, it does more damage than good. I've come to realize when someone seems angry with me and I question myself and what I must have done to deserve such an emotional beating...and then I realize it's not me at all. I know it's a difficult concept to grasp when you're feeling insulted and hurt but, once you start to really adopt this concept, you're perception of life, pain and forgiveness changes. Remember...when you hold a grudge or hold on to anger it's like trying to stab them, when truly the only wound will be on you. To not forgive and move forward is never going to take you where you want to be. I promise you that. If someone attacks you, your lifestyle, your work etc., it's probably a level of envy, disappointment in themselves, fear and, quite honestly, a closeness to you they share with no one else. We say

it, we sing it, we think it....we always hurt the ones we

love. And our truest friends understand why we're upset

and never deny you forgiveness and on the level of best

friend, doesn't expect an apology at all and just patiently

waits until you're ready to talk about what's bothering

them. Is there a level of narcissism in a person who's

putting you down...yes. The curse of that word and the

meaning is about a myth of a man who thought he was

so perfect and beautiful in every way, that he spent all

of his days staring at is reflection in the water. He grew

closer and closer to admire his perfection...only to wind

up falling into the water and dying. Keep in mind, if

you've forgiven someone but, realize that the

relationship has reached it plateau, it is perfectly ok to

keep that forgiveness to yourself and just let the

unhealthy relationship rest in peace. Forgiveness sets us free. Apologizing for being wrong sets us free. And to quote one of the 12 steps....only apologize as long as it causes no harm. For instance, no need to say to your best friend that you've been having an affair with her mother or father, as the case may be. That might cause I slight rift. Remember this one thing, we all wear masks. Hundreds of them throughout our lifetime. They change with the personalities we deal with. Only you know who you really are and if you're having a hard time figuring that very thing out, it's time for you to disappear into "you land". You will never truly love anyone, be a true friend or even an active family member until you know who you are. We are all given roles to play....keyword is given. There is going to come a time where you decide you don't want that shitty role. Black sheep, the wild one, the drunk, the perfectionist, the

caretaker...whatever it may be. It's right then and there

that you're able to choose the role you want. Not

everyone will like it...some people might downright hate

it. Believe in me when I tell you my delusions of

grandeur about getting sober were naturally, if I got

well, everyone around me will be happy and no one will

have to worry about me anymore. They'll be no more

drunk dialing, texting, emailing. I won't be unpredictably

nasty or scary. Everyone can relax. Well, I'll tell you

what, I lost just about every friend I had. The ones that

stuck around were just happy I was happy and enjoying

life for the first time. The others had their issues. But I've

learned to try not to personalize everything. I mean

c'mon, we're human. If someone runs up to you and

yells, "GO FUCK YOURSELF, SKANK!!!" You might, ya

know, feel kinda like, you know, like maybe....punching that ninny in the face. Before you're arrested on assault charges, give this one a shot. Smile confidently if not slightly cocky, nod at them assuringly and be on your merry way. For the rest of that day if not the week, that person will quietly wonder all day every day what the hell was that? To their friends they might do that street, side cheek Sylvester the Cat type laugh and high five each other, because people do frequently do that, I've found, when there's nothing else left in the realm of responses. It's a fun way of shouting out "we're stupid and clearly cannot respond with any sort of dignity, so we'll slap each other's hands abnormally hard and double over with cartoon laugh. And as the day progresses, every time someone brings it up, we'll slap the shit out of each other's hands again. Maybe even snap our fingers with each other to add that extra bit of stupid! We've all been told since childhood that if someone hurts us, knocks us down both physically and mentally, if they mock you, ostracize you, make you feel like shit and sends you home sobbing....it means they like you. What the hell kinda nonsense is that? So, the extra hard someone kicks me after knocking me into a puddle means they really wanna be my life partner? If that was the case, for all the times I felt bad leaving school, I should have a harem. That is all nonsense and a cop out on acknowledging bullying. Stop saying it and stop doing it and address it. Being knocked around does not mean, at all, that someone desires your hand at the 8th grade dance. If you listened to your kid a little closer, teachers, this one goes out to you to, do not dismiss the child by telling them such ludicrous malarkey. Generally if a bully is created, a bully is a lifelong member. Here's the upside....I was bullied in school. I'm very lucky that all 8,000 times I thought I would have liked to die or worse, actually tried and thankfully failed, I realize it was the smaller part inside of me, crying out, "um, heellloooooo.....we don't all agree here Schmitty. How about you and your brain take a nap, while the rest of us formulate a plan to prevent you from killing all of us!" I knew on my final attempt, which was closest to success, that I was sacrificing the best of myself for the worst in other people. Aside from the first time they hear I died until I'm in the ground, I'll fade to black and be little more then an ice breaker between two mutual friends, starting with, "oh my God, did you hear what happened....?" While the other person gasps in disbelief and says, "Oh I know! It's terrible! What happened?!"

And that other person will proceed to make up a totally false reason why you're out of the game. My punishment would have been to stand there and listen to something ridiculous like, "well, I heard she lost a ton of money on the slots then got crabs from a prostitute and was too embarrassed to face the day." If this thought ever crosses your mind, it is not you making this choice. It's a part of you that's been hurt. Being very hurt is all consuming but it's not all there is. Beg and scream for your real self, rational self, wonderful self to wake up and tell your hurt self, I promise this will pass. I promise days are ahead that will be magnificent. I promise you'll love and be loved again. I promise we'll laugh again. Please, just give us a chance. If you've been left by the love of your life for someone else, if you've lost your job and have 3 kids. If you lost your home and have no place to turn, life will not be this way forever. The person who left you cannot be forced to love you. If they don't and you still do, it's hurts. It sucks the life outta you but, get this. Chances are, if you're an adult, it's not the first time you've loved someone and even if it is, eventually, if that person leaves you be, soon every morning you wake up doesn't start with them. Certain things will remind you of them but, it won't linger like it used to. Maybe it'll make you happy. That would be beautiful. Maybe it'll piss you off. Either way, it'll go away quicker than you think. If it bothers you, it would behoove you to talk out loud to yourself....I've also found that's a good way to monopolize a sidewalk, so it's a win win. Tell your brain you've had enough. I recommend fantasizing sexually about your therapist, the girl or guy behind the counter of the pizzeria, someone who's sitting across from you on the train, bus, and caravan. It's a decent distraction.

As we know, I generally hang onto the therapist.

## Me and my hot therapist

There's a class we take in counseling that refers to transference and counter-transference, which very simply means either the client reminds the therapist of someone in their life or the therapist reminds the client of someone from their past. Hopefully it's someone good but it's certainly not all the time. Visually my therapist looks like similar to my ex-wife. Before sitting with her, I was sure I'd do nothing but fight with or put her down. She said she thought I was a soccer mom. If you've ever seen me, you know I couldn't look any further away from a soccer mom. As of the time she had met me, I had a short sleeve shirt in which unveiled quite a few tattoos and a lip ring. I'm pretty sure biker boots and ripped jeans. I guess soccer moms come in all shapes and sizes. To this day, we both still refer to me as "soccer mom" I'm a big fan. She could call me a dickhead if she wanted. I'm not altogether sure she could say much that would offend me but this isn't a challenge. I obviously have a therapist because a few things bother me. People who know me might think I'm a little sensitive. Comparably I would say....like a newborn in a tanning booth for an hour. That sounds really awful and cruel but it surely is how you could explain my emotional sensitivity. Fortunately, I'm able to wear many hats. The second I'm on the clock, you could electrocute me and I'd tell you that ok. I'm not terribly hurt. Could you hand me my fingers? That all being said, the first 18 times I professed my love for her, she explained this theory and

I convinced myself she was making this up to make me lose my everlasting love for her. She was unsuccessful. Inevitably the counseling had to come to an end because that part of my therapy had plateaued and it was time for us to break up. Well, all these years later, I still hold her diamond ring in my top drawer, waiting for her to stop her nonsense and that ugly word "heterosexual". I need to know what the statute of limitations is on no longer being seen as a client. Especially since now I'm more like a colleague. I have a decent idea that's she's onto me and since I'm keeping it just between you and I, I know my secret's safe. If you feel like you wanna have a petition made up and have 3 billion of your closest friends giving the ok nod for me to no longer be seen as a client, please feel free. Humorous as this is, she has positively no romantic interest in me whatsoever. I just like to convince myself that she does. The majority of my relationships went that way. Jesus, I'm not even sure if half of these women I called "girlfriend" even know who I am. As it stands now, I'm in a whole new environment and have my shit together. I'm hoping that raises my stock value.

Psssstttt.....but if you do feel like getting that petition rolling, far be it from me to stand in the way of your dreams.

## Chapter 3

Sometimes I think God is like a sadistic personal trainer – shows up at your house at some ungodly (no pun intended) hour in some cheesy velour sweat suit, ridiculous head and wristbands with an enormous "G" bling on both. He yells hyperactive bullshit at you like "GET IT UP!!!! YOU GOT IT YOU GOT IT!!!" You know damn well you're running and lifting beyond your means, but deep down you hang on to the notion that your inner body will be "bangin" if you listen to Him......that being said..."WHAT ELSE YOU GOT FOR ME BIG MAN??!!!! BRING IT!!!"

Life smashes line drives at your head, and it's not when you're focused and standing, knees bent, hands on knees, glove on your hand watching the plate...no sirreeeeee. It's when you're standing at the snack shack

with 2 dollars in hand waiting for some shitty, soggy grey

hot dog with far too much sauerkraut that's only going

to fall into that nifty little hot dog specific holder.

Unassuming...fantasizing about how after you eat this

hot dog, you will not allow anyone to speak too closely

to you and how you'll burping up this madness clear into

the wee hours of the morning chomping antacid.

Yep..."should I get a soda? I mean do I have enough

money...let me check my...*CRACK* (not even paying

attention to anything else but your saline popping meat

bi-product) Bam! 10 seconds of utter shock and a quick

grip to the back of the skull....the brain racing

with,"What the fuck was that??!!!" Next is the sound of

an overzealous, scorekeeping mother yelling,"Oh my

goodness!" "Oh my Goodness?! You dumb bastard I just

got nailed in the head with a baseball, and you say goodness?!" (I think in my head, because that's kind of harsh to yell at Carol Brady, even though I did reserve the right after being pelted in the side of the face. Life...and its pleasant little surprises.*sigh*

Naturally I'm talking about falling in love (well not naturally, because it could be that I'm getting an absurd bill tomorrow I can't pay, but for today...it's that fancy nancy little notion called falling in love). The wonder of losing complete control over any rational thinking you thought you may have had. Granted, sometimes it's a real hoot, and very little work and naturally, fully reciprocal. That fantasy notion sounds nice, right princess? I used to be a big blah blah believer in,"if you're really in love, it's not work." And then I turned 13. Being an adult and meeting your "match" is exactly like that...igniting a fire. Fascinating to look at, keeps you warm, heats up your leftovers on a stick, but can burn the living shit out of you and remove and/or destroy all your photo albums and pleasant little knick knacks that really don't mean a thing, but are irreplaceable and it annoys the shit out of you. Your friends are like the insurance company that tells you, "I told you that you shouldn't have left that pizza box on top of the stove. On or off, that bastard was bound to catch fire!!!" Yeah, thanks, genius...any other snippets of "told you so" in that bag? There's nothing like falling in love with someone who appears perfectly normal on the surface and turns out to be an emotional trampoline. It's like having a clock radio you particularly enjoy, and one day it stops working. No warning, no real reason. You check the outlet, you smell for burns, but nothing seems to pan out. You gently take it apart, and look to see what's broken, and carefully replace it. For one fleeting moment your precious little alarm clock turns back on. You leap with joy, and just like that...silence. You have no idea what the hell you did to fix it to begin with, so you have no idea which part to pay attention to. Maybe it works perfectly again for about a month or so...if you're lucky you might get 6 months to a year, but then all of a sudden...silence again. Deep down you know there's no part to fix anymore, and that clock of yours has to go into wanting, experienced hands that know how to fix it...and hopefully you find a new one...eventually.

I might have had my heart broken. So what does that mean? Suck down a bottle of pills and wait to "fall asleep"?

Then I would have missed the sound of my father's shoes shuffling back and forth 8 billion times an hour after a snow storm, asking me more than repeatedly, "Sar, have you seen this? Whoa...lot's of snow...Sar? See it? Are we getting more? Sar, you listening? Wow.....snow." I might roll my eyes and attempt to block him out, but deep down I realize how lucky I am to have someone that longs to talk to me as unbelievably often as my father.

**The Chapter after the last one.....**

We're not kids anymore, ya know. Maybe some of us are in happy marriages, single...dating like we're 15. Ah who's to say and no one is to judge.

Recently I was asked by a respected, wise family member...what are you? I guess a lot of people wonder that about me. Do I think of myself as a mystery? Nah..I'm not that interesting.

Do I identify as a homosexual? I guess. I prefer women. And then I'm labeled. I identify as nothing and everything.

I don't have an answer for this question other than this....

I'm a 35 year old woman..I guess I'm fairly attractive, and my sense of humor is dry by doable, I'm smart enough to tie my own shoes. This is what I want for my life:

Stand 100 feet from me in a crowded room...watch "Paul and Mary Jones" do something completely ridiculous, and look at me. Look up at me with smiling eyes and an unassuming grin. Elbow me under a table when "Rita" says something so completely off the wall, no one gets it. Interrupt your conversation because you hear a song playing you know I love to ask me to dance.

Cut a piece of the dinner I didn't order to let me taste it without asking. When you walk away from the bar, have both of our glasses in hand and expect the same from me. Try To "hustle" with me when 70's music comes on even if you absolutely have two left feet.

Know when you make a sandwich at midnight, that even though I said "No I don't want one...."I'm so going to eat half of yours.

Pick up my shirt and smell it when I'm not home because you miss me.....know that I've smelled yours 100 times. I don't care if you spoon me. I don't give a shit if you tell me I'm pretty...let your eyes do that. I'm not a kid. I don't want a gender....I want a companion. Someone that gets me. I want you to laugh at and with me for no reason. Someone I know beyond a shadow of a doubt will stand there when I'm gone, and feel lonely. Not because they're alone, but because they lost their best friend. I'm at no age and no stage to be picky....but I will be anyway. Drop to your knee and promise me a life of imperfection and mess. Promise you'll be my best friend forever. Promise when you make love to me, I can see the love in your eyes even if you're a little fresh and want to be a little rough. Promise you'll come home and tell me the truth because you trust me enough to know that you're human. Promise me that when you look in my eyes, you'll know exactly what I'm thinking...Label me as nothing other than your partner...in every way. I'll count you as my number one blessing as long as you extend me the same courtesy.

What did I tell that family member? I'd love a

companion. I'd love eyes to look at me across a room -

eyes that tell me everything I need to know.


Just to love. And for that.....there will be no ropes on the

neck, no pills down my throat, no gun to my head. Just a

smile and a deep, relaxed sigh.

## Ok....another Chapter....kind of

Since you wouldn't know unless I told you, it's Christmas time. What better time to reflect on failed, miserable relationships and exes you'd like to sneer at for being happy. How dare they!

The variety of, ugh, beautiful people I've been blessed to sleep next to at night. The never-ending nights of staring at the ceiling thinking, "If you snore one more time, I am going to lay my body across the pillow I'm holding over your mouth. *sigh* - in any event, I'd be lying if I didn't say I'm old enough and mature enough to look back and miss that snore. Well, some of them.

Would it be my first love that traveled 1600 miles to be next to me? The one I laughed with, danced against like no one else existed. Had some of my most passionate experiences with? Who was the single most beautiful thing I'd ever seen in my life. The one whose heart I broke in half over a terrible mistake? The one I see now as a successful fighter I admire and secretly, well not so secretly, I hate for not loving today.

Maybe it's the aforementioned workaholic – spoiled me rotten in the area of comfort, but I was too young, too high on pills and too damn ignorant to appreciate her willingness to give me a beautiful life. Prove to me that I was clearly the smartest person on earth...and is hugely responsible for my typing as we speak. The overly distracted "wife" that answered the phone with questions like "HOW'DJA DO??" When clearly you did nothing and are too confused to not answer the question with things like, "Fantastic, hon." The type of aesthetically foxy woman that is so consumed by business that she clearly forgets that SHE called YOU and yells into the phone, "Look, I have 15 things goin' on right now...you have to call me back!" And you're left holding a phone against your face for 17 seconds wondering what the hell just went wrong with that conversation.

I sometimes thank ignorance for not allowing me to get married because I would clearly be married and divorced, let's see...to the incredibly compassionate, wonderful teacher, the very sexy, fly by night bartender, the high school sweetheart that I now have the finest love/hate relationship on earth with. It may have been the incredible friend I made for life that separated us because of the 22 year age difference. These wonderful women took care of me...emotionally, physically (sometimes) – and I'm sure each and every one breathe easily that I packed a bag and walked off into the sunset. In any event....thank you ladies. I wouldn't be the unnaturally sociopathic character I am today without you.

## Sex and the mechanics of a '79 Oldsmobile

Sex is a funny topic... Fact is, as of today's date, I haven't been touched by anyone other than myself, actually no....not even myself in 2 years. Quite possibly more but,

I lost track after the absurd amount of roughly 6 months.

Live and learn. I've never been promiscuous. A tease?

Yes. But not much of a one night stander. The few times

I've done the "no attachment" thing, it's been with a

friend...or at least someone whose first name I knew

well.


I've learned some things about myself during this period

of celibacy. You see, it's not that I couldn't find a sex

partner if I wanted to. Fact is I've learned to have some

odd thing called self respect. I went through that

beautiful phase of trying to fit in when I knew deep

down I was gay. I did that "try to be popular" thing when

I wasn't popular at all. Only to find that giving the

impression that you're easy is not the way you want to

fit in at all. The chances that our innocence could have been ripped out from under us because of a stolen Playboy or a deck of cards with various, very difficult looking positions and 976 numbers (back then, they were free...and they said things on that phone that made virtually no sense to a grade schooler. We just knew it was dirty) was great but, for whatever reason we realized on our own this just wasn't the right thing to do. Spin the bottle was still nerve wracking and innocent. 7 minutes in heaven was still 6 minutes of nervousness in a dark closet and 1 minute of some slobbery mess that was supposed to resemble a kiss. After that kiss was over, generally the boy would "ask you out" which is a less douchey way to say "go steady". Now, here is where the 4 hour long pre-adolescent phone conversations would begin. Proclaiming lifelong love after being together for 2 days....here is where the questions begin. "Can I go to second base next time? I love you. I won't tell anyone. It'll be 5 seconds. Don't you love me?" Ok, I think. What's the big deal? I do love him with all my heart and I know I'm only 13 but, I know he's the one. I'm going with it because this is clearly going to be my husband. So, he starts to go in for the Second base kill and begins to squeeze them like perhaps they were going to make a honking sound.  Now he's panting like an animal, which makes no sense to me because that was about as sexy as tying my shoes. Even still the idea of boob honking seems to make even grown men grunt like cavemen. Maybe it's the simplicity of being able to turn a man on so easily that turns me off a bit. Women aren't much different once you know what you're doing but the challenge is certainly more prominent. I longed for love. I wanted someone I could be sure would be my date at every prom, dance, function, life...someone who would walk me to class and kiss me goodbye. Be waiting by my locker to leave together. I've had asshole boyfriends who used me for rides to school in my '79 Oldsmobile. The beautiful Olds that fit 47 people comfortably, went from 0 to 60 in 3 days. Had the original tires and windshield wipers....this was 1992. Why you would purposely want to climb into this death trap with the thumbtacks holding up the material on the ceiling...the playboy bunny lock covers, a radio that was laying on the floor attached to what looked like 4,365 wires, no knob and the hope and a prayer, you'd be able to push a button in such an obscure way, it might land on a working radio station. The backseat had been violently pulled forward by my brother (the previous owner) in the event that he had locked his entire baseball team's equipment in the trunk built to fit 647 spare tires...all of which were flat. 2 spoked rims. An aircraft carrier and a partridge in a pear tree. I any event, when you sat in the back seat, your head was painfully pushed forward. The driver's side door was from a different car, so you had to climb through the passenger seat to unlock it. Above my leg to the left was a very expensive equalizer...it made the "benzi box" really crack your head open with the bass. This was not hooked up to floor monster, but I often fantasize about being able to blast Edie Brickell as I fish tailed into the parking lot. Aside from this crackle of lite fm who seemed to take a real fancy to playing the same 3 songs for the whole day. I believed the DJ was a drunk and was constantly passed out on the panel. Regardless,

I was happy to have some tunes lasting through my asbestos lined speaker holes. The car had to have the break applied while revving the engine simultaneously, when stopped at a light, or it would stall and life would become unmanageable. If there was a slight chill in the air, I would have to start my car before I took a shower, dried my hair, maybe put on makeup, but not often, put on my school uniform in order for it to be driven. Make no mistake, during this preparation, I had to go back out and start that car at least 5 times. Before you started it, you had to "pump the gas pedal". It harbored this very intense smell of vanilla because my very guido brother generally hung air fresheners from the thumbtack heaven as well as the vanilla pump spray. Basically you could smell the inside of the car...from a classroom on the other side of the building. On my last night with my beautiful wheels, I took a turn and the entire axle

snapped clear in half and I screamed toward the picture

window of a laundromat and came about 6 inches from

mowing down an entire family, poor Sadie...that was her

name...rest in pieces. I bought a white t-top firebird,

complete with a black bra and a lovely Phoenix type

drawing on the hood. While sitting in a car with 3

smokers who had magically ran out of cigarettes, didn't

realize that's every time I try to turn the car over, the

fuel pump had split and the car was surrounded by

gasoline.


After that I roller skated everywhere I went.

And the asshole boyfriend who used me for rides to school....is still an asshole today.

And I found someone to stand by my locker....she was my whole world. We thought positively nothing of walking each other to class and giving each other the casual peck on the lips like the heterosexual couples did. Either nobody seemed to mind or we really cared so little, that we didn't even notice. I had finally experienced what reciprocal, open love was. We did the whole, uh...Juliet and Juliet (how else can I describe it...she wasn't a Romeo dude and neither was I) us against the world routine. We made promises no one on earth can keep. We stared at each other nauseatingly for hours. We were excited to walk through the West

Village and realize we could hold hands without anyone judging. 3 weeks out of high school we got our first apartment together and I have to admit, I think I did better responsibly at 18 than I do now. In any event, it was a wonderful memorable time in my life. I suppose I'll always have some fraction of my heart set only for her. She was the first love I'd ever had who didn't give a shit who thought what...she just wanted to be near me as much as I wanted to be near her. We were young, we did foolish things out of just a world of curiosity.

It was also the first time I tried coke and started experimenting with hard drugs...sorry, let me rephrase that...it was when I fell in love with coke. And not the beverage but the powdery white shit that you suck up your nose, rub on your gums, like the key, the spoon, the straw, and then tear the bag open and suck the residue out of that only to sadly look around for more. It made me talkative, full of energy. It tastes like gasoline and turns you into a maniac who cannot shut up AT ALL and think that a perfect stranger really gives a fuck why your mother decided to name you Sarah. They so want to know your plans on how to fix the fiscal cliff and are fascinated by the fact that you chose Bank of Cadillac Bumper because they gave the best toasters. Fact is, if you haven't tried coke, don't bother. It might feel good....but it will definitely turn you into some form of an asshole. That I can guarantee. Let's not get this mixed up though...the coke and my first love have positively nothing to do with one another other than that was the age I first tried cocaine. Got it? Good.

I love the smell of vanilla air fresheners still. I love the thought of my first love still, minus any of the not so good parts….I hate cocaine. So, all in all…It would seem my brain is aligning the way I'd always hoped it would.

Sometimes when you try to make sense of certain memories, it gets very foggy and it's almost impossible to have a linear thought – and then one day you smell a vanilla air freshener and you remember what that first kiss with that first girl meant to you – and everything just aligns itself. Give yourself a minute.

## Where I come from....literally

I'll hear the creaking of the wood floor above me...more like a "creak...swish, slide, creak, shuffle, and slide, creak..." The loud creaking of the steps. Some louder than others. The loudest I've memorized so as to attempt to sneak in slightly after hours. I never really had a curfew so the point was usually to sneak a guest in by making it sound like there was only one set of feet. The world's most impossible house to sneak around in. Anyway, I sit in the dark, around 5 am, having my coffee, watching the news. Thinking how unbelievably nice it is that I've just woken up after the cool 2 or 3 hours of sleep I've gotten, providing insomnia didn't totally have its way with me. I wait to see whose creeping down the stairs at this hour. Sometimes, if my mother had a particularly creep-o nightmare, she'll get up at some absurd hour to tell me about it or if it's a big day for me, she'll creep down to wish me luck. My father, on the other hand, will stand in the doorway of the steps leading up to my bedroom, to yell into a room my mother is sitting in playing her 458th game of bejeweled that night, about some political statistics that really only make sense to him and the Secretary of Homeland Security. Now, my mother will never say, "Arthur...step INTO the room so Mount St. Helen doesn't wake up and come downstairs and yell at us both...until Mt. St. Helen (that being me when I'm woken up during the hour and a half I'm actually able to sleep) erupts, runs downstairs and acts like I'm going to yell, until I realize we're not big yellers, so I'll walk quickly with a little bit of a stomp, not slam but, shut the bathroom door with enough vigor to get my point across...reopen the door almost immediately, shuffle stomp past them and then stomp up my stairs while murmuring, "I'd like to see how YOU'D like it if I started talking about why the field of harm reduction is so important at 5am....blah blah blah....!" He will then continue to not just drop his shoes on the floor but, as far as I'm concerned, holds them up over his head and drops them for maximum bang-age. He'll continue to pace back and forth through that second floor hallway repeating, "Tri, you know?! You know what I mean, Tri?!" And in my head, I'm yelling, "GODDAMN IT....TELL HIM YOU CAN'T BELIEVE IT!!! WHATEVER THE FUCK IT IS, YOU ABSOLUTELY CANNOT BELIEVE IT!" But nnooooo....not my mother. She'll sit there with a completely clear conscience. She will not even flinch about the idea of either never answering you or waiting a good 37 seconds before she sllooowwllllyyyy answers you. Where I have been brought to a point where I have to say, at the end of every sentence to her, "ANSWER ME!" That will speed her up by 8 seconds. The other day, I told my mother to do me a favor and turn the car on so it's heated up when I clean the snow off. However, as simple as that may sound, I must tell her this way:"Mom, please go outside...put the key in the ignition, turn the dial to defrost and hit the separate defrost button, turn the dial toward the red...away from blue." "Why am I doing that?" "Because, it will make it easier for me to clean the car off." So, I go upstairs and get my snowsuit on and I'm ready for business. Where's mommy? I go outside...to the very compact Celica, which is blocked in completely by my father's Crown Victoria. Quite the opposite of a compact. So, my mother's car is completely surrounded by the house, a 14 foot hedge that is at least 4 feet deep and my father's unmarked police car. I go over to the driver's side door and pull the handle, "oh shit, she locked the damn keys in the car with the car running. Wait, that's impossible...I think...let me dust a little of this snow off of the window so I can see if.....so I can see my mother, seat pushed just about all the way up to the steering wheel, seatbelt on and her purse next to her....with the radio blasting, wispy little hairs blowing in the heater breeze....locked in." Now, I have to knock gently because she responds somewhat skittishly...somewhere along the lines as if I was banging on the widow with a chainsaw while wearing a mask of, well....human flesh sewed up into a pretty face. She'll grit her teeth and give me an,

"ooh...you fuck! Fucking scared me..you fuck!" My

father's gotten her to throw hot coffee onto herself a

few times out of fear. At least now she can understand

the delight of what it feels like to be sent INTO A

HAUNTED HOUSE RIDE ALONE!!!! Another fun hobby my

mother used to have. Pretending she was going to get

into the cart with me when entering a haunted house

and then jumping out at the last second as I'm going

through the dark, plastic curtain, on my own, AT 6 YEARS

OLD!!! Horns honking, wind blowing and cardboard

monsters popping up in your face at 6 is worth at least 2

more years of therapy. There she is, aiting there for me

at the end, cracking up. And if it wasn't that awful

haunted house, it was a carwash. Do you have any idea

what it's like to feel a car start rolling, by itself, while you're in the backseat of the car, drifting into blinding soapy water slapping itself against the windows with such force, it sounds like the windows could break?! By the time the carwash ended, I was paralyzed on the floor saying the Pledge of Allegiance because I couldn't think of Our Father and just figured that's close enough! Sadist. Woman had me watch the Exorcist at 8 years old. I slept in bed with her until I was 29, I think, and the first night I decided to be a big girl, my lovely brother was hiding under my bed, waiting to push it off the ground the second I started to drift off. Did she show sympathy when I yelled out that clearly some creepy little bastard Regan was under my bed?! She sure didn't! I have no sympathy. Anyway...*tap tap tap tap* "What are you doing in there?" "What?" "WHAT ARE YOOUUUU DOINGGG!?" "What?!" "OH FOR CHRIST'S SAKE!! OPEN

THE WINDOW!! *hard imitation of rolling window down* she finally, very slowly rolls (and even though it's an electric mechanism, she still manages to get it to roll down even slower...it's a talent.) "Are you talking to me, Sar?" "Am I yelling into one window at one person who happens to be behind that window?" *she stares at me blankly* "Why are you sitting in the car?" "You told me to warm it up." "Right, just turn the car on, blast the defrost and come in the house. Why the hell do you have your purse?!" "I didn't want to leave the car running with the keys in it and you were upstairs getting dressed!" *blink blink blink*. Mom, your car is blocked on all 4 sides and the chances that someone's going to decidedly sprint into your house, hoping like hell no one's in there, to grab your purse at 2:16pm is pretty slim." "Oh, ok. So, should I bring my purse in or do you want to bring it in?" The whole conversation took place through a 2 inch crack she was good enough to open for our communication since I'm the one standing in the freezing snow and she's in the shoebox with the heat on volcanic. I guess it's worse that I appease her by continuing to shout through the crack the 87 times she said, "What?!" To me. "Well, you can bring it in. You don't have to stay in the car while I clean it off, ma." What does she do next?????? You'd better believe she turned the ignition off, grabbed her purse, locked the door and took off for the front door. At this point I feel compelled to ask, "this isn't the first car you've ever been involved with along the lines of cleaning it off right?!" "Why? I can't shovel, Sar. My back has....." "Yes yes yes...I know about your back. Just hand me the keys." "Are you going somewhere?" "Yeah, I'm gonna floor it in reverse so daddy's car gets blasted into the street. Maybe tie some rope to the hedges and rip those suckers right out so if I ever need another getaway plan..I'm all set! I won't touch the house, though because there's enough of a draft. Old house..lots of drafts." She proceeds to stand there staring at me as if this plan of mine could actually occur. Mind you, if I bumped into my father's car with a cotton ball, I'd be ejected from the house. Crash into it? I'd be removed from the will.

So, back to the dark, early morning shuffle I hear and the overly loud creaking of the steps presents my father. He looks a lot like he purposely made the most extreme faux hawk in existence. Rocking the slightly oversized

Jammie pants, generally a white tank top..also slightly larger than is necessary and a faded, green flannel shirt. I look at him and say absolutely nothing. I have the coffee cup maybe about half an inch from my mouth, which is open, waiting for some of the coffee to go into my mouth and most of it to spill on whatever shirt I decided to destroy that morning. Yes, occasionally, if I gulp a certain way, some liquid will sprinkler system itself out of the lip piercing. I all need you also to know that, even right down to the hair, the faded flannel, the oversized pants, tank....I wear just about the exact same thing as my father. Except I will eventually tie a bandana around my head because let's face it...you never know who might see you at 5am in your pitch black living room.

So there he is....made it to the very bottom without incident. He doesn't look at me at all. I, however, am staring at him with so much anticipation, I could all but dump that cup of coffee right into my lap and save myself the trouble. He looks left toward the front door, he looks right toward the kitchen...left turn means he's going to question if I've locked the door in his OCD kinda way. Right head turn means did I unplug the coffee pot and make sure no stray grounds got into the sink...because heaven knows, maybe after 45,674 years, enough coffee grinds will surely clog the sink eventually. Still no movement. No indication of what weird rule I had forgotten to follow that morning. Don't get me wrong...he's not a dick about it. He just likes things a certain way. So, if I have to spin around three times humming, "Mary had a little lamb...." Before shutting off the light, then who the hell am I to break up his party?

Well, he begins to move his arms a bit so now I'm wondering if he's sleep walking. The notion scares the shit out of me. Never mind the creepola zombie like walking but the thought of having to wake him up and him blasting into action. So now the hands, balled into a gentle fist start doing little side to side motions....."It's bananas....B A N A N A S......it's bananas......B A N A N A S....." Turns right back around after his little dance and song and climbs back up the creakfest steps, creaked along right into his room and trampoline creaked back to bed.

I was 15 minutes late to work that day....because I was frozen with my mouth agape, coffee cup just slightly below my mouth...wondering if my father was truly possessed by Gwen Stefani or if this was some strange new rule I would have to abide by every morning that I wake up. Sometimes the thought of living alone just bores me. How will I live without my father's vocalized pause "applesauce"? You know he has a lot on his mind when he keeps repeating the word "applesauce". Some days he'll just walk around saying nothing but applesauce. Why? We don't know and we won't ask so you're on your own with that one. When he REALLY has a lot on his mind, he'll blast classic dance R & B....and keep saying, "HIT IT!" Which means no matter what you're doing, you must stop.....and dance. So, for all of you who know, for instance..."I specialize in love..I'll

145

make you feel like new...I specialize in lloovvveeeee....let me work on you...." By Sharon Brown (excellent song, by the way) you know for sure that song is going to be cranked just enough to possibly have a neighbor call 911, wherever you are, you'll have to stop and boogie down. Speaking of which, my father asked me, not too long ago,"Sar, how can I hear a song on the Internet without being arrested?" And yes, even though you'd stare with confusion at him, I, on the other hand, don't even flinch anymore. And I went ahead...I did...I introduced him to YouTube and when he discovered you can really listen to any song in the world, it took him about an hour and a half to be standing in Best Buy reading off speaker brands asking me which one is the best...because not only did I introduce home to YouTube, I was really gonna give him a thrill and hook up the cheapie speaker set I bought for my iPod. Now he

knows that you can make a nightclub out of your laptop,

there was no way he was gonna settle for anything less

than speakers that also came with a woofer. Yep...he

bought a set with a super woofer. He danced around the

kitchen that night to the same song over and over and

over ....it's a one hit wonder by a group called LAX

..because that certainly doesn't train your brain to think

of a stool softener at all. I wonder if that had anything to

do with it becoming the wonder that is a one hitter. I

any event...I can't think of the title of the song,

ironically, after listening to it 400 times. He kept trying

to inch the volume up slowly, thinking he was getting

one over on my mother who pretends to be deaf. It was

like a mother yelling at her teenager to not blast the

new toy he got for Christmas. "ARTHUR C'MON!!"

"Alright, alright, I'll lower it (for 8 seconds and then

slloowwwwllllllyyyyyy inch that woofer knob). The next

day, he carried it upstairs into the bathroom with him

while he took a shower...and I guess he thought that

because he was in the bathroom with the door closed

and the shower running, we wouldn't have to suffer

through LAX another 12 times. He sure didn't hear Tri

baby yelling through the door..clever little applesauce

he is. He was sitting at the kitchen table one day with his

toy, yelling up to me in the attic, "Sar, what's that band

with the black guy who sings? Ya know, he sings and

there are white guys...you know, there are like 2 guitars,

drums...the black guy...?" "Dad, you're gonna have to go

a little deeper than that. I mean, I'm good but, I'm not

that good. What do they sing?" "Uummmm....he's

singing to a girl or about a girl." "Do you hear what

you're asking me? The band has drums and guitars and the black man sings to a girl...or about a girl....Jesus, I don't know, man.....Hootie and the Blowfish." "HOOTIE AND THE FUCKING BLOWFISH, YES!!!!!" This is the point where I lower my head and think, "yes, the time is coming for me to branch out on my own. It's only a matter of time that I start waking up, singing , "they call we Wanda, they call me Jill, they call me Sasha (I obviously don't know the real words to the song but that's what makes it so much more colorful) that's not my name, that's not my name.....that's not mah......name...". So, after my winning musical group guess, I now listen to my father, for the next 4 hours say, "Hootie and the booty....Sar, Hootie and the BOOTY?! Hoooooooootie and the booooooooty.....(that last one you have to sing as if you're mocking someone...like na na na nnaaaa naa na! Get it?") Well....for about 3 days,

we strutted to Teena Marie, we bobbed our bobble

heads to Bob Marley...and we now "don't wanna wait

innnn vaaaiinnnnn for your lloovveeee" Bob Marley

fans..you will now be singing that all day. Non Bob

Marley fans, that song has been remade at least 12

times by 12 different artists...except Hootie and the

booty and since Hootie dropped his booty and sings

country, chances are he won't remake "I don't wanna

waaiiit in vain for your lloovveeee..." Unless maybe he

can add some twang to it and REALLY remake it. I think

country is the only genre that hasn't remade it. We have

it in, obviously, reggae, slow rock, Annie Lenox (because,

let's face it, Annie has a genre all her own.) Hootie, I

double dog dare you....I don't want to wait in vain for

YOUR love!! And neither does my father. We allowed

him to play LAX 4 times maximum with a 2 hour wait between each. Even though, secretly, I was singing it all damn day...and still don't remember the name of the song...lyrics are something like this, "At the risk....of being a male chauvinist..." Then I draw a blank and make up my own words. I caught my mother snap her fingers and rock her shoulders at least twice so, secretly we were enjoying LAX too but we couldn't rescind on our schedule rule or the song would be repeatedly piped into the whole house. No one would ever leave without being addicted to this one hit wonder. I waited for my father to yell, "Hit it, Sar!" while he was doing his shimmy thing behind me, every time I had to wash a dish because this nightclub was in the kitchen. So, being the fairly good sport that I am, I shook my shimmy and snapped my soapy fingers, which is no easy task my friends. It's like whistling with crackers in your mouth. I bopped around and occasionally yelled the lyrics with him. I figured, "hey, why not make dish washing an event?!" My mother would occasionally walk into the kitchen...shuffling, rocking her hard posture (which means her shoulders are so relaxingly forward, I have to yell at her to stand up straight, like she's a 5 year old in a military camp) he'll yell at her to "Hit it!" And do you think she does? You bet your ass she does. And make no mistake, they'll shake it till the song's done. I like that at any event, minus, of course, a funeral, (unless it's warranted...some people want a party at their funeral. I know I would.) my whole family is out on that dance floor. I'm not too sure if my brother would "hit it" at my father's command. I'm not sure my father would command him. I'll have to test the theory next time he visits. My sister in law would "hit it" and yes, I realize it now sounds risqué but, I know what I'm saying, I've explained it to you...so let's stay on track. Today it happens to be snowing so, by the time I get home from work....YES, I GOT A JOB!!! A REALLY GOOD ONE....WE'LL BRIEFLY DISCUSS IT ANOTHER CHAPTER!!!! Anyhoo...I'll get home, I'll be in the door for 1.2 milliseconds and he will ask me no less than 18 times how bad it is outside. He'll find multiple ways to ask me...and he will sound like an auctioneer. To an amateur, you would not know what he's asking but, because I'm anticipating it. "Sar, isitreallybadoutthere?isitslippery?shouldishovel?areyou gonnashovel?isitreallycomingdownoutthere?isitcoldlikei sitgoingtofreeze?isitsticking?howisitoutthere? All of that will come out before I even remove the key from the lock. My mother will rock the hard posture down the stairs at slower than a snail's pace. I'll say hi to her and she will take 26 seconds to process it and then say, "hiya dolly! How'd it go?" Another person who can ask me an open ended question so I have a variety of ways to answer it. So, before I get my coat off, because I always wait out my mother's long pauses (which cause her to rarely get in any trouble, because she rreaaalllyyyy thinks before she speaks). Today, I'll remove my really goofy woolen cap (I love getting older. There's a certain age you get to when you realize it's better to look like a 4 year old with a pom-pom hat and be warm, than try to look cool and freeze your ass off. I got this hot looking hat just about pulled over my eyebrows and a coat on that makes me look like Randy from A Christmas Story..."I can't put my arms down eehehhhhhh..." Let me give you a snippet of what goes on in my house during a blizzard when we're snowed in. We're all antsy and just over each other. My mother and I will settle in calmly and watch a movie.....my father on the other hand, can't stand the silence so it becomes a battle of the minds that we've lost.

Snow shoveling...our neighbor snowblew (made up word, because it sounds better to me than snowblowed) our entire sidewalk and driveway (because we have awesome neighbors and I'll admit, at the risk of sounding cocky but I'm allowed to feel sexy once in a while. The 60+ grey haired, dreadlocked, cool, smooth, charming fella across the street thinks I'm pretty...so my parents have me to thank for the snowblew. So, he only has the stairs to sweep and the cars to dig out. Which never happened...read on) "Sar, should I wear a scarf? Do you have old gloves? Is it too hot for a scarf?" "No, dad. It's not too warm for a scarf." "What about gloves?" "Um, no. You absolutely can't EVER shovel snow without gloves." "Old gloves or new?" "What? What does it matter if they're old or new? (Why am I even asking this?) whatever's more comfortable for you, dad." "How about this jacket? Or is this one better?" (Now I've stopped answering) should I start with the steps or the cars? Can you do one car?" "Yes, I'll even do both cars, dad." "We'll, when?" "After I have coffee." "We'll, when is that?" "It's whenever I finish...I don't have a coffee timer (see, now I'm letting him win. I'M GIVING IN!) "Do you think it's gonna snow more, Sar?" *crickets* "Should I call Hecto?" "Who the hell is Hecto?" *he walks out the door...damn it....first round I totally lost.*

Set the scene *mom and I are sitting in the living room eating salads, watching Jeopardy...in walks your buddy and mine* "I got this bread. Wait till you see this beautiful bread I got! I went to Trader Joe's with cousin Paul...and I got this beautiful bread. Wait until you see it! Do we have sauce left? I'd like to have this bread with some sauce! *the questions are coming at a rate where you absolutely cannot jump in and answer...he walks into the kitchen where the sauce is heating up*" DO WE HAVE SAUCE LEFT, TRI?!" "Dad, it's right there on the stove." "IT'S ON THE STOVE?! BECAUSE I'D REALLY LIKE TO HAVE SOME OF THIS GREAT BREAD WITH SAUCE! DID YOU SEE THIS BREAD I GOT?! *I'm gonna win this round..I am NOT going to ask him how we could have seen this bread if neither of us are in the same room*

"Oh, good there's sauce. Is it hot?" "It should be, Arthur. Stick a fork in it." "What should I do, taste it?"*mom looks at me and shakes her head...and refuses to respond again...leaving me to battle him on my own* "WOW, YOU GOTTA TASTE THIS BREAD....I GOT AT TRADER JOE'S! SAR, YOU KNOW HOW MUCH I PAID, FOR THIS BREAD....AT TRADER JOE'S?! *mind you..the space between the living room and kitchen does not warrant shouting at all* "No, dad. How much was the Trader Joe bread?" "OH MAN, YOU GOTTA PUT SOME BUTTER ON THIS BREAD AND TRY IT! IT'S DELICIOUS! I NEVER WENT TO TRADER JOE'S....ON RICHMOND AVE.! I'LL GO BACK THERE, YA KNOW...WHEN WE NEED BREAD! *right, because that's convenient from West Brighton* "THAT OBAMA, HE'S PHONY! IT'S ALL A FACADE! WHAT ARE YOU GUYS WATCHING IN THERE! COME AND GET SOME

OF THIS BREAD!" *my mother and I look at each other for a good ten seconds...and simultaneously go back to looking at the TV, crunching away on our salads. There really was no way to win that round. He didn't give us enough of a chance. Bad sportsmanship*

My mother is very tiny. Very. She longs to gain weight and if the doctor scale says 112, she's excited because she gained those 12 lbs. She loses it quickly and, yes, I know the common idea is we wish we had that problem. I do realize, though, that it's frustrating to her so she'll say wonderful things like, "Sar, do you think my pants grew? I think my pants grew." Speaking of doctor's offices, my mother gets very nervous so more often than not I'll join her....for one particular reason. What she doesn't realize is that in her angst, she will start F

bombing left and right. Not at all common of my mother

to do. It goes a little something like this:"Ooh Sar, I'm

fucking nervous! Do I have to fill out all this fucking

forms? Can you get my fucking card out of my fucking

wallet! I'm fucking thirsty....do you see a fucking water

fountain? Excuse me miss, what the fuck does this mean

on the back of this fucking form? Do I have the fucking

sign? *then she goes is...on this particular day, she was

getting an epidural for back pain...I knew if I wasn't

there, they'd arrest her for public lewdness.* "SARAH,

THAT FUCKING HURT! YOU SAID IT WOULDN'T FUCKING

HURT! ARE YOU FUCKING KIDDING ME!! *child no less

than 6 sitting in front of her doing the little "find game"

on the last page of a Highlights magazine....her leg gives

out from the shot. At the very last second, I grab the

front of her coat and throw her on the couch..she begins swinging her leg back and forth. She's moving her leg, bending it at the knee* "OH MY GOD, SARAH! IS MY FUCKING LEG FUCKING PARALYZED?! HOW THE FUCK AM I GONNA GET OUT OF THIS FUCKING OFFICE?! I THINK MY LEG IS FUCKING PARALYZED!! *10 times I've shushed her while pointing a blinking neon sign at the child. She's basically moving her leg like she's doing the Charleston and repeatedly yelling that her leg is paralyzed. As a daughter, I did the only thing I could do.....I laughed so hard I almost peed my pants. I laughed the entire way of carrying her out the door, driving her home and carrying her up the stairs and laying her on the couch...payback for sending me into a damn carwash by myself* "WHY ARE YOU FUCKING LAUGHING?! MY LEG IS PARALYZED! LOOK AT IT!!" *now she's doing the "Alley Cat. I'm still laughing so hard, I can't quite get out that her leg is, in fact, not paralyzed. If you've been in my company when I REALLY laugh...I do this unusual eeehhhhhhhhhh kind of noise in between the guffaw*

My father is unbelievably smart. I wouldn't object to saying he's a certain kind of genius whose mouth can't keep up with his brain. If you asked my father the most obscure question, in a second, he would answer. My mother is a different kind of genius....she listens sometimes way too well. She doesn't flaunt it but, if you asked my mother something about life in general, advice if you will, you'd have your answer...and would be right. She's a tiny woman and while I know everyone out I'll really wonder if her pants grew....we do realize pants don't grow. At which time I'll inform that pants do not grow and she'll wait a few seconds or more like 34 seconds (no less than 34 seconds for any response and it could be a pause as long as 79 seconds. Once I waited one minute and 48 seconds but she had a cold so I let her pass) she'll laugh a kind of sinister laugh even though she's not being sinister, she just laughs like that. So for about 2 months straight she'll eat a pint (or a half gallon but who's counting) of ice cream. After those two months, she'll grab the half inch of weight she put on and say, "no more ice cream for me. I can't stand having this belly!" 4 or 5 days will go by, she'll have a stomach like an 18 year old (two kids this bastard had and I look like the one who carried them) and she'll be bringing the spoon up to her mouth....sinister laughing.

See, my mother will be fantastic with you...if she likes

you. She's been known to put "whammies" on people

who have wronged us all as a family. One guy made fun

of her in high school about having buck teeth (which she

no longer magically has) he fell off of his motorcycle and

*drum roll please* lost his two front teeth. One guy in

Seaside (that's where the "shore" is for all you out of

towners) took advantage of me as a youngster and sold

me an "unbutton my fly" (popular way back when I had

big hair and long nails....I didn't get the contract on no

long nails for lesbians yet. I was in the dark about it) for

$60.00. Basically more than my entire paycheck stocking

shampoo at Sav-on. She went in there and demanded

my money back. They argued and then she got that

"whammie" evil kind of smile face...next day....that

store, which was connected to a long line of stores,

burnt down to the ground. Neither building on either side had a mark on it. Other things that have been "whammied" I'm threatened with a miniature whammie....which means I'll get a stuffy nose or something. I hate stuffy noses so you'll just have to wait till you're in the "in" crowd and she'll creep you out all on her own. Good to have a whammie capable mother.

I have an older brother...whose cheeks are growing redder and redder just from feeling he has right now that I may write about him. Well, he'll have to get a cold rag because he's gonna be part of this "not really" masterpiece. My brother and I are polar opposites. We do look somewhat alike. I suppose if I grew a goatee, we would be twins but I just don't have the time or patience to sculpt such a masterpiece. He's a good man. He's an excellent father and I suppose we'd have to ask my sister in law for the final verdict but, I'm pretty sure he's a decent husband. He's very well put together on the outside. By that, I mean he's the kind of guy you'll see wearing a sweater vest and tie on casual Friday. Quite honestly I think my brother wears a sweater vest to bed, in the shower, to play touch football. He's not afraid to stand in the kitchen on a holiday (in his sweater vest and tie of course) and possibly an apron if it's one of his fancier pastel sweater vests. (Easter and the vernal equinox deserve pastels). I suppose you could say he's a metrosexual. Very concerned about looking well polished. So not your common garden variety jock that has to be told every 3 days to please take a shower or snap his fake front tooth in when he goes to a wedding. Chances are that same gross man would have to be told to brush his teeth and take a shower. Arthur Jr. is a tremendous athlete and much like my parents, seems to always be in very decent physical shape. I'm the only one in my family who can very easily become a tub-o. If I eat a candy bar, by the last bite I've packed on 26 lbs. My family could eat a bag of Halloween candy and lose 8 lbs by the last MaryJane. He was a professional baseball player but his dream, really, was to have a family. Yes, he preferred the concept of having a family over playing sports professionally. And he is a TREMENDOUS athlete. He's also very handsome so poster boy Yankee? Indeed, yes. It was an awesome sight to get to Ohio, where he played ball and see people of all ages waiting in line to get his autograph. So he lived a dream and now he's living another. My brother is the type of guy who asks many questions and I don't mean in a healthy, inquisitive way. I mean things like, "what are you taking?! What are those?! Aspirin?! Why are you taking

aspirin?! Do you NEED aspirin?! And what are those?!

(I'm guessing the big yellow bottle with Bayer on the

side and the even bigger jug that reads Tums on the side

was a great mystery.) Antacids?! What do you need that

for?! Why are you taking those?! You have a stomach

pain?! Why do you have a stomach pain?! Did you do

something to get that stomach pain?! Why do you have

such a big bottle of that?! Why are they all different

colors?! Do they do different things?! The different

colors?!" Now, much like my father, all of those

questions are asked in rapid succession so, there really is

no way to answer them. Basically he is answering all of

those questions on his own and for whatever reason he

is absolutely disgusted that you have a stomach ache

and a headache and wants to know why. I've been sober

for 2 years and yet he's convinced that I'm getting high off of acetaminophen and antacids. I wonder if I take enough if I could hallucinate or laugh uncontrollably or vomit enough to get head spins. Once, admittedly, I had a glass of red wine 2 Christmases ago at his house. I didn't hide it. I didn't pretend it was soda in a pint glass. It was a glass of red wine in a wine glass. He asked me what it was and I told him and he didn't really say much....until we were in a packed gym and my nieces basketball game with every person we've ever gone to school with since birth with my youngest niece on his lap. He began to loudly ask through gritted teeth and a magenta face, "Why were you DRINKING on Christmas Eve? You know you shouldn't be DRINKING! If you DRINK, it will break my heart. Absolutely BREAK MY HEART IF YOU ARE DRINKING DRINKS OF RED WINE IN A

WINE GLASS ON CHRISTMAS EVE!! I can't believe you were DRINKING DRINKS THAT YOU SHOULDN'T BE DRINKING when there is alcohol placed everywhere for everyone but you to be DRINKING DRINKS OF RED WINE OUT OF THE RED WINE DRINKING GLASS YOU WERE DRINKING WHEN YOU WERE DRINKING THOSE DRINKS that could make you DRUNK if you had more than that one half glass of RED WINE THAT YOU WERE DRINKING OF RED WINE OUT OF THE RED WINE DRINKING GLASS YOU WERE DRINKING FROM! YOU BROKE MY HEART!!!"

Needless to say, I considered punching his head off. We're emphatically non violent people but I thought this would be a good opportunity to see if I could knock someone out in one punch. Then I realized this may be the reason he has my niece on his lap to act as a shield from me punching his face off. Now my niece is upset because all she heard was that I broke her father's heart. So, while I gritted my teeth and had many quick retorts like, "wow, how'd you even notice after your 9th beer or 5th glass of scotch. Fact is, I had positively no idea how much or even if he drank. He may have had some wine or a few beers He may have had a bottle of scotch. But you can't fight fire with fire if I'm holding fire and he's holding water, get it? I could have done the adult tantrum and said, "I'm an adult I'll do whatever the hell I want when I want it...who are you to blah blah blah...!!!" Or, "it was one glass of fricken fracken wine. You're acting like I killed someone!" Granted, I was angry and rightfully so. It was an inappropriate setting and he shouldn't have embarrassed me or put me on the spot like that in front of so many people and especially my niece. Fact is, once I got a grip I realized his rant was coming from a good place and in time my niece may remember that conversation, she may not but, she will be a teenager one day and we know what teenage years bring. Wine coolers and the like. Well, they were wine coolers when we were too young to drink the drink out of the drinking bottle when we drank or drunk our drinks. Scary shit now like energy drinks mixed with what seems like crack cocaine mixed with moonshine in a pretty can that looks like a non-alcoholic beverage that makes you speak Creole mixed with whatever they speak in Paraguay and Nigeria mixed. I only know this because in the throes of my alcoholism, I decided to buy 2 of those delights. Now, I was a DRINKER who, yes, drank the drinks out of the drinking glass that we drink from when we drink, A LOT. I could polish off one of those fancy gallons of wine with the tiny little finger handle for a ginormous gallon jug and still speak to you.

Mind you, I spoke gibberish and said things like, "how come you don't call me when penguins dance?! Puppies were everywhere and I can't find my ice skates! You're an asshole!!! Don't call me ever again!" Now, I won't slur and I surely won't remember it...but I'll say it! And most of all, I'll believe it's right and you're gonna get screamed at if you fight me on it, so choose your battles. One of my best friends used to get the really fun brunt of my works of art and she would entertain me until she could slip in with a, "gee, Sar, you know I love you and I wanna talk all night but I have an awful headache and I really have to lie down. How about I text you in a bit if I feel better? Does that sound good, you pretty pumpkin who is my very best friend who I'm giving a great big hug to?" Brilliant, right?! She was unbelievably brilliant because that would make me feel warm and fuzzy all over and because I felt so loved it would prevent her from getting some delightfully happy text like, "DON'T YOU DISMISS ME!! YOU THINK YOU'RE TOO GOOD FOR ME?! YOU THINK YOU CAN JUST THROW ME AWAY LIKE TRASH?! FINE!!! GO AHEAD....LOSE MY NUMBER AFTER THIS!!!" Only to be followed up 18 seconds later with a hysterical call of me crying so hard you can barely hear beautiful snippets of things like, "you kknnoowwww my 4th grade teacher beat me to a pppuuulllppppp....she beat the poor kid behind me so bbbaaddddd...he would throw up on me every mmooorrrrnniinnnggggg.....she was a nnnuunnnn.....my godfather NEVER llooovveeeedddd mmeeeee....I had to put my ddooogggg to sleeeeeeeppp....." "oh My God, what?! When, Sar?! Oh that's awful!!! When?!" "Seven yeaarrsssss agooooo!!!!"

By her telling me I was pretty and loved and wanted to be hugged she bought herself the whole rest of the night aside from an occasional text that would read, "I'm so glad you're my BFF...you uunndeerrssttaaannndddd me..I love you so much!!! I'd do anything for you!!! If a shark had you in its mouth, I'd punch it to death!!" Entertainment at its finest. And she was just never the kind of friend who would be kind enough to tell me how pretty and entertaining I was the night before. She'd somehow just understood that it was best to talk to me kindly about being worried about me during the 4 minutes of sobriety I had a day. When it really starts to get frightening is when the drinking has gotten to a point where no one knows you're drunk anymore. Where your behavior seems perfectly normal. You're driving, you're shopping, and you're giving other people advice on how to be happy. Telling everyone how good it feels to be sober and that you wished you spent more of your days like this and today is going to be the start of it! And in your mind, because you only had 4 beers that morning, you feel like there's really nothing wrong. If people understood the kind of anxiety you had, they'd never dream of expecting you not to drink. If you had medical benefits and could get proper medication, you wouldn't need alcohol. That's the answer....once I get back to work and get my own place I won't have the same time for this. Not to mention thinking no one in an office environment would smell you coming from miles away. And even if you have the presence of mind to realize you can't stink going to a job interview instead help yourself to a few pm's...your choice, Advil, Motrin, generic, etc. Vicodin, Percocet, Roxie's... (hilarious. I just typed in Roxicet and the spellcheck changed it to Roxie's....that's the world we live in) would wake me up. Significantly. And ironically, I got more comments on how pretty my eyes looked when I was high on any type of opiate. I felt limber, happy, energetic....I could clean a house (really well...REALLY WELL) in 22 seconds and then go out and buy all the neighborhood kids ice cream while putting on my Sunday best and caring not about the dirt stains I would get from falling over due to the earth's shift and not at all my completely botched equilibrium after haven taken more than an entire bottle of prescription pills before morning coffee. The reason I would fear not the grass stain is because I would get higher the next day and find some combination of toothpaste, wood cleaner minus the oil that would make a forever stain...disappear! See, we didn't have too many opioids available that we readily knew of way back in 1927....or 1990. Whenever high school was. I'm sure had we checked our parent's cabinets, most of whom were nurses, we would have never even had to learn how to roll a joint with one hand on the dashboard while driving to some dark, dangerous place to smoke it. Kids these days don't know how easy they have it. They can completely mangle their lives by going no further than their bathroom cabinet. UM, PARENTS.....TIME TO WAKE UUUPPPPP.....IT'S 2013 (at this point) YOUR KIDS ARE TAKING YOUR PILLS AND THEY ARE GETTING ADDICTED TO THEM AND ARE GOING TO HAVE A REALLY HARD SHITTY TIME GETTING OFF OF THEM AND THEN THEY ARE GOING TO TURN INTO SOMEONE LIKE ME AND YOU DOONN'''TTTT WWWAAANNNNNTTTT TTHHHHHAAATTTTT!!! Amazed...I'm utterly amazed that there are still parents out there who don't realize that ALL of their painkillers didn't grow legs one day and skip off. VERY BIG PROBLEM PEOPLE!!! WAKE UP!!! I will become teenage public enemy #1 and call them out. YOU COULD BE YOUR OWN CHILD'S DRUG DEALER …..THINK ABOUT IT!!!


Anyway...off track....my brother and his DRINK THE DRINK LECTURE...it came from the right place and when looking into the glorious eyes of my 5 year old niece at the time, I realized, if I keep this up, I may be the person she comes to if she's ever afraid. Afraid because she drank, afraid because one of her siblings drank, afraid because she got in the passenger seat of a car with someone  who had been drinking and thought maybe it would be uncool to tell that person to go scratch their ass and get out of the car because they're drunk. I do explain, fairly often, to a now 6 year old, a nine year old and a 5 year old that no matter where they are, no matter what time it is, no matter who they are with, they can call me and no questions asked, I will come get them and take them home. I wonder if they sit and think about maybe one of their basketball pal's mom, blazing through a red light and yelling from the back seat, "THAT'S IT MRS. BLOW THROUGH THE RED LIGHT!!! I DON'T HAVE TO TAKE THIS SHIT ANYMORE!!! PULL OVER...I'M CALLING MY AUNT!!!" *ring ring* "Hello?" "Hi, Aunt Sarah. It's me." "Hi you! What's up?" "Can you come pick me up?" "Sure honey, where are you?" "Remember that time when I was 4 or Aidan was 4....maybe Olivia...and we drove passed that clown? It's not there anymore. But if you go toward that place where they sell those clothes and I liked the pink shirt but Maku (yes, they call my mother Maku, like she's some Lion King character) said it was too loud so, we went to shoot water pistols instead?" "Ashley, you lost me at Maku. I have no idea where the clown that isn't there anymore is.....rest assured....BUM BA DA DUM!!!! (Superhero entrance sound) I will find that damn clown that isn't there anymore and I will bring water pistols. You did tell me to bring water pistols, right? You can't miss me .....I'll have the loud pink shirt on that says Maku on the neckline! What happened? Did Mrs. Frickenheusen get drunk? I mean, I know you're all 9 but, that might make a carpool mom drunk! Drunk? As in she took you guys to get beers after school because the ice cream parlor was closed?" "Aunt Sarah....I'm just gonna get back in Mrs. Frickenfracken's car. You're

taking too long and I'm too young to drink beer!" In any

event, I will drill this notion into their head day and night

until they're old enough to realize that's Mrs.

Frickerfracker's daughter is a drunk and shouldn't be

driving. Yes, I'll drive the young Frackthefricker home

too, don't worry.


My sister in law, God Bless Her Soul....she either answers

456, 906 questions a day or she knows how to be

perfectly silent at this point and realize there is very

little sense to my brother having to ask, "why do they

call it heather instead of grey?! Should I not wear

heather?! Should I search for grey?!" Sure Mr. Pink

SweaterVest ....hunt for that manliness!! I any event,

they're the couple who host just about every holiday...even the made up ones. They sneak a kiss from each other in the kitchen, well, when everyone in the world is watching because we all seem to habitually crowd into one corner no matter whose house we're in. She's the kind of mom who never misses a game yet works her ass off both in and out of the house. She's a smart girl....like creepy Jeopardy smart. She's not creepy...but she's that kind of smart. I'm pretty sure her and my father could play trivial pursuit for 8 days straight. She's not a snobby kind of smart....she's a chill kind of smart. A glass of wine and a laugh kind of chill smart. Fact is....she deals with DRINK IN THE DRINK OF THE DRINKER GLASS DRINKING!!

**I don't think I understand the basic rules of chapters....but here goes another random thought....**

I was recently thinking about the sexiness of adolescent crushes. This chapter might get a little racy, so feel free to just whip right over it (I just tempted you beyond repair and you just can't wait to read fresh things....way to go, trooper!!! It's on!")

At 14, I was, and proudly have a remained...a true to form geek. I sported a classy mullet, rocked the oversized sweatshirts and really should have never thought it was a good idea to apply my own makeup because I looked remarkably like I put paint can on a table and smashed my face into it. I sat behind who is entirely responsible for me saying for the first time in my life (even though I had known since I was 6), "Oh, I am sssooooo gay." Perfect 90's enormous hair, fire engine red lipstick smeared onto the most perfect mouth I've ever seen. The smell of perfume that seemed to linger in my self made bubble every second. A cheerleader no less...and smart to boot. The very moment I understood the capacity to really want to sexually jump someone was the moment in art class she slid me a note on her circus stationary saying, "I had a dream I was making out with my boyfriend, and when I opened my eyes...it was you." YOU HAD A DREAM YOU MADE OUT WITH ME??!!! OK, so not only does my crush appear to want to be friends with me, but seems to also share my interest. I didn't realize that at the time, and just chalked it up to her being silly and not really knowing my ravenous need to be near her.

She took me in willingly and decided I would be her project makeover. We spent endless nights applying coral Maybeline to my mouth, feathering my hair to my awkward little face and pretending for her sake that I really lloovvvveeeddd New Kids on the Block. Joey Joe is ssooo cute *please kiss me you sexy cheerleader screams in my head*.

It started off slow. I wouldn't say it was this dorky notion of, "let's practice kissing for boys." Let us enter the bedroom at the end of the hall, shared with the older sister I prayed NEVER came home. School clothes strewn in the corner. Posters of "Joey Joe" covering every bit of pastel wallpaper. My cheerleader putting on tremendously romantic slow songs…walks toward me in a way that lit my body on fire. "Dance with me." And here I am. Lightning blasting through my skin..slow dancing with the most beautiful girl on earth. Bringing her perfect face to mine, close enough that I can smell that red lipstick still today. Breathing into my mouth, and knowing she absoloutely owned me at that moment. Breaking away from me with a perfect teenage coyness. This fantastic teasing went on for a full year….until we discovered a bar that charged $5 for a glass that was never empty.

13 beers later…and some crazy emotional, "WHHYYY MMEEE?" breakdown (because that's what we do as teenagers) that made absolutely no sense, my perfect best friend begged a stranger to get us home. Because she was so incredibly hot I think this boy would have

driven her to Quebec if she asked. In any event, we roll

out of the backseat and driver Bob looks at my

cheerleader and expects a "thank you"...she basically

laughs in driver Bob's face and pushes me clear onto the

ground. Good shape. "Let's sit on the extreme slope of

grass in front of my house and looooook at the sttarrrsss."

Here rises one year of angst and desire. "I'm not going

into the house until you kiss me." Not even one second

or one word of fighting me, and the great love of my life

leans in. Let me try to explain to you what this does...

This kiss will forever rank as the one moment in my life

everything made sense. I had waited my whole 15 years

on earth to feel this girl's mouth against mine. It was

slow and perfect. She wasn't giving in...she was

passionate. Stopping my world from spinning by not

shoving her tongue down my throat, but moving into me

delicately. It was a hungry, overdue kiss. The perfect separation, and now we're sober and we're going in the house, and I'm positive I'm going to break down the door, my parents and anything in my way like a linebacker to get the hell up to my bedroom because it is so on!

Ah, yes...let us remember that at 15 years of age, it is tremendously difficult to get in and face the parents that are wide awake on the couch in the living room. They'll say something like, "Whoa...how was your night?" And I'll utter some genius snippet like, "Wewenttothemovviiieessssand Igottagetta bbeedddd." That makes sense. I'm practically knocking her down to get upstairs and get at this not acknowledging that my parents are staring at me and my brilliant description of our night with their mouths agape. My love has to do peepees so I'm gonna bounce off the doorway and plug in my romantic, teenage, wall draped Christmas lights and pop in a mix tape to get the mood right. I let out a whispered, "yyeeessssssss", and my door opens. There she stands and I'm ready. Slam that perfect girl into the door. Mouth wide open now, starving for this moment I've waited so long for, and what happens?

Shove. "Sarah, that's enough. Satan has taken over your soul and you need to pray. BE GONE SATAN!" What the fuck?! Did we not just? Were you just out on the lawn with...and you're yelling I'm possessed? I thought we were in this together? Did I not just feel your precious tongue in my mouth? Where the hell is Satan in you, sister? "I'm going to bed. Get on the floor and pray for Satan to leave you!" When the hell did Cary White's mother enter your body?

Bet your ass I slept on my commercial carpet...praying for Satan to leave me. Beaten.

22 years later...my very best friend, my cheerleader, married to a wonderful man who busts his ass to take care of his beautiful wife and two beautiful children. She is my confidante and my guardian angel, and still my closest and dearest. You might be asking if the sexual tension still exists, and I'll tell you this...No one will ever be my first true teenage love. Nothing will replace that kiss, and I believe since then, I managed to pray the devil out of my soul. Maybe. I will never love another person as much as I do my cheerleader...because she is my best friend. The sexual tension...went to bed went I removed those Christmas lights from my bedroom wall.

**I don't like to stay on track too much....in case you didn't notice.**

It makes things get way too deep. That and the chronological button in my head broke in some sleigh riding incident. It was on a hill called "Dead Man's"...very tragic. Everything else is ok aside from a complete inability to stay in step with time. At this point I'm over 2 years sober, have a fulltime job....still live in the parent's attic but at least I can shop for apartments now with high hopes.

Better believe 3 chapters from now, you won't know if

I'm 38 years old or 15. Godspeed.

**In every workplace....**

There is...

A bitch know it all who files grievances about the toilet

paper being upside down

One super nice person who aims solely for you to open

up to them and freely complain, so they can blackball

you at a moment's notice

One dingbat who's been working there for 8 billion years and yet still has no idea what he/she is doing

One perpetually lazy person who manages to get away with doing about 20 minutes of work a day

Some dipshit who thinks he is far too hot for words and that no one is bothered by his incessant sexual harassment because "no doesn't always mean no"...and you know you want it. He will follow you into the copy, break, bath, billiard room every time you even motion that you're going to get up...so you, in turn, must become a ninja in order to get paper for your printer.

Always one who thinks no one knows they are a not so functioning alcoholic and the overload of body spray is not covering up the rancid vinegar smell coming out of your skin.

One who will pretend to go to the bathroom and continuously "just take two puffs" on a never ending, horrifically smelling, butted out generic brand of cigarette.

Always one who is just as bubbly as can be all day every day and you wonder if it's because they practice severe acts of torture on each other nightly.

One who makes an absolute scene and asshole out of themselves at the holiday party.

One really vicious supervisor who won't budge while never steering clear of telling you how stupid they think you are...and one incredibly nice boss who lets you get away with murder. Watch for the latter of the two because they are building up a war of "they take advantage of me" in their head. At least the vicious one is rotten to your face.

One who will act like your mother and perpetually be there for you....so she can also tell the other "mom on board" the deepest secrets you're sure would have been incredibly safe with her. Live and learn kiddo.

One person who seems to morph into various co-workers as the weeks go by. Will continue to ask "what are you doing for lunch?" Even after the last 4 years of making up that you're going to meet the pope for coffee, your dog, who was humanely euthanized 2 years ago, died. Because it is the truth, it's just a past truth. You don't know how many times you've used this excuse so you begin to wonder if she thinks you're a serial dog killer. She will cut and dye her hair like yours, start speaking like you and feel all too necessary to gain your approval.

Generally the dingbat will be really hot and see nothing at all wrong with bending over in either direction in front of you....hence why she still has her job.

You will always have a supervisor of some sort, withhold vital information about how you were supposed to do something so they can step in and act as a hero and fix it....because they're scared to death of your intellect and ability to take over their ship.

You will always have one person who's been with the company since before the company even started. In fact, I believe they came with the building. They won't retire because they hate their spouse and are convinced of the superstition that almost immediately after you retire, you drop dead. This person can either be the hardest working or do no work at all...fact is, they won't be fired because they've been there just too damn long. Usually they will make less pay than some 20 year old ninny running the switchboard. They don't care because their frame of mind is in the ice ages and don't realize that minimum wage is no longer $0.02 cents.  Everyone will see fit to buy this very person some sort of Christmas present because let's face it, if you're in with 60 year Steve, you're good to go. The bosses respect his opinion and respect even more so that he had positively no desire whatsoever to be anything but a mere clerk of some sort.

There will always be titles made up like Facsimile Supervisor, which colorfully means you check the fax machines, staple the shit together and hand it out accordingly. The manipulative boss will make up this title so you feel prestige...and won't ask for a cent more. He'll even get you a small box of cards with this title on it but you'll be too young to realize how utterly douchebagged out you seem proudly handing out a business card with that title. But you just rock on with your fine facsimile self!

There will always be one person who constantly has bad breath.

One person who gets their nails done 3 times a week on their lunch.

There will always be a hidden affair that is oh so not hidden, going on behind some random closet door.

There will always be one woman who wears the glasses with the the dip down arms, attached to a neck chain with a very obvious piece of scotch tape holding one side together. She eats peanut butter and jelly or tuna/egg salad every day for lunch and wraps it in one of those old fashioned, flip the top over and hope for the best sandwich bags. No ziplock for her...she could just as easily reuse the same piece of overly yellowing masking tape. She drives a car that has rust that runs clear through the floorboards and it is never a year that is over '86. She will barely speak to you and is probably an excellent worker, although her social skills are that of a wet towel that was left on the lawn chair overnight. This woman is filthy stinking rich...eternally single. Could have had at least 14 new pairs of glasses covered by insurance but feels it's frivolous because hers work perfectly well. Even though they were prescribed 27 years ago and now she is almost legally blind. She keeps her hands on the 10 and 2 while driving a cool 18 mph and still swerves at the last second to miss a pedestrian...and whispers very gently while turning the wheel hand over hand so slowly at just the last second, "ooooohhhh.....sssooorrryyyyy" she spends the majority of her money on her beloved cat who has a human name like Paul or Kevin...because he is her one and only lloovveerrrrr. Keep a safe distance...this woman generally smells like peepee and hasn't brushed her teeth in a while. It's not necessarily that she has bad breath but she will always have shit in her teeth. She just doesn't see a reason for personal hygiene. It's wasteful. She's also ferociously protective of her office supplies...if you quickly swipe one paper clip out of the 1446 she has in her magnetic clip holder...expect to pay hell.

There is always one jerkoff who will very blatantly pass your idea off as theirs.

One who will ask you for a ride to their home an hour away, even when they know you live 7 minutes door to door. You will always drive by this person standing on a bus stop in freezing rain without a hood or an umbrella...and ALWAYS get stuck at the light RIGHT next to them. You can pretend you're texting or on the phone and you don't see them....they still think you're an asshole so don't waste your acting skills.

There is always one who has headphones on so loud that they might as well have concert speakers on their desk. More than likely they'll be listening to music that you despise and will suck their teeth and mumble under their breath when you finally politely ask them to lower it. Even though this has gone on every day for one year straight. That person is usually in customer service and is responsible for handling phone calls...of which he takes one a day and it's usually to his mother to yell at her for not bringing money to him. This kid usually does data entry at a machines pace and he's young, so an onsite, low maintenance computer guy. The boss will keep him on anyway so don't waste your breath. He'd sooner let the kid have a whack at the computer and destroy it then "waste" his money with an actual professional.

There is always someone who rifles through drawers looking for something to steal

Everyone steals pens...so that doesn't count

There is always some girl on her phone all day arguing with her boyfriend. What you don't know is that it's probably a new boyfriend every week and they're arguing because she's a clingy psycho dying to get married.

One will constantly claim they have very serious health issues....I made the mistake of ranting and raving out loud at a job a very long time ago about a woman who would always do these hard, dramatic wheezes when she was late and perpetually called in sick...I went on and on and on and on....and she died. 20 years later, I still beg for her forgiveness. Had I kept the eye rolling to myself, I'd have felt a lot less guilty. That's the kind of dick I am.

One will always call out because either her kid/dog/cat is very sick and they need to get them to the doctor as soon as possible. Not only will this get them the day, they think, but also a resounding, "aawwwwww"

It's not too often you get this character but every once in a while there will be that stupid ass who calls in sick and then comes to meet their co-worker friend at work for lunch.

Several aalllwaaayyyysssss on Facebook updating what a dick someone around them is, not being smart enough to realize that 10 other people within that office are getting simultaneously notified of your insubordination. Good luck with that, champ.

There will always be someone who brings in the stinkiest dinner leftovers, heat them up and eat them 3 feet from you...at 9am. This bucket of food will be slowly picked apart throughout the day, so get used to going home with a curry suit.

There's someone who should have been fired 12 billion times for various, very serious reasons...but you know, deep down, they have beautiful dirt on the boss...so not only does this chicken head keep her job but she also gets raises and probably a "little something to hold you over" every week.

There's always someone whose accent is so thick, you are utterly clueless as to what they're saying and you'll generally, involuntarily stare at them with your mouth open while they speak. I suppose the brain thinks if we open our mouths, we'll understand better. If we try to answer them, we have a tendency to shout our response because clearly if you're screaming at someone who actually speaks English, however with an accent, your message will be loud and clear. They're asking you an open ended question like, "how was your weekend?" And you will shout things like, "RIGHT I KNOW!"

Always a tremendously overweight girl who thinks she can squeeze into a size six. Her pants will reveal her ass crack no matter what she's doing. She will wear low cut at the top and short cut at the bottom shirts with a push up bra for these abnormal mountains and will flirt with every single guy who comes within 400 yards of her

while she picks tiny little crumbs off of her muffin and

just about pinches the pieces into her mouth. I suppose

this is to give the impression that she eats right and is

only that big because of the thyroid issue she never

stops talking about.


How about the person who perpetually either has white

shit in the corners of their mouths (as I stop to

simultaneously, obsessively tear at the corners of my

mouth 800 times a day). Or that delicious lip sweat that

is never wiped off. It's not like it's in a difficult place to

wipe. Sleeve over the mouth if necessary dear. Generally

this person will have an odd, sweet, pungent sweat

smell. Usually this person is the mook who follows the

97 year old owner of the company who refuses to retire.

Lip sweat bodyguard.

There's the quiet mystery worker no one has ever spoken to.

Sometimes a receptionist who's a snitch and thinks she holds the power. Meanwhile this person speaks so unprofessionally, you wonder why, first, she's not canned or moved to a position where she must be silent and, B, people don't hang up immediately and go to a competitor.

Always someone who goes home fired up about you. Someone in that office thinks you're a dick and they hate you. Your name to them is a Pavlov theory or "Canadaaaa Fallllssss....step by step...slloowwllyyy I turn...." You send them into a frenzy so make sure you go out of your way to be overly friendly because that will drive them to homicide. Hopefully someone in life pisses them off more than you so you have a good running start.

One has a psycho husband who calls 400 times a day to scream at her for not answering his texts. She gets out of work at 5...he pulls the car into the lobby of the building at 4:45. He doesn't work. He's addicted to painkillers and meth. He's incredibly paranoid and will never be convinced that his girlfriend is not cheating on him. As a matter of fact, she refuses to use the ladies room because she might miss dickhole's 342 phone call. She will not be attending the holiday party.

How about the one who has copies of biblical quotes all over their cubicle. That person generally has a glamour shot with their boyfriend...they're wearing white shirts, jeans and crisp white socks...the woman is on the floor on her side, leaning on her elbow with her legs stretched out, looking like she's leaning on him. He's sitting up with the one knee high Indian style with his hand casually draped over one knee. She also has loose leaf paper tacked to her cubicle with crayon drawings that

look more like crayon scribbles from her 2 year old
niece.

Lest we forget the Hello Kitty collector...where their desk looks like a cartoon character exploded. Everyone takes the easy way out with this one if they've gotten her as a Kris Kringle. All you have to do is get a basket of Kitty's scented erasers and you're all set. They'll squeal with excitement and line them up in front of their monitor. Next to the Hello Kitty stapler, tape dispenser, which has no use at all in the office because what the hell are you taping, pencil holder and sharpener...jackass pencil case that's made for a 6 year old. If they're really warped, they have the lunchbox with inner thermos to keep their cup o' soup warm also on display. Basically the desk looks like a pink nightmare. This person will take a job as an "acting supervisor" which means they'll be doing the job of a supervisor while still making Hello Kitty pay because it is quite obvious that this 33 year old with a 6 year old mentality is a dingbat. If you happen to be the Hello Kitty dingbat, take my advice, get a box and clean off your desk because it's not cute...it's ridiculous.

Usually someone whose desk is such a dusty disaster, has a yellowing picture of Garfield or the kitty hanging from the tree branch that reads "hang in there". This was hung when the person started their job in 1986. They're not aware that Garfield is 112 years old and needs a break. At this stage of the game, that picture has been up so long, if anyone takes it down, the whole cubicle will implode. She also still has August up on the calendar and it's November. You don't wanna get stuck walking behind her because you'll flip the fuck out because of not only how slow but zig zagging as well so you can't get around her. When you say excuse me, she will just silently move to the left and never say a word. She also smells like peepee and generally wears the same outfit every day and she doesn't give a shit what you think, first. Secondly, she doesn't even think you notice. The amount of crumbs layering inside of her keyboard could make an entire loaf of bread...family size. The keys are sticky from God knows what...and the keyboard itself is a beautiful yellowish brown. If you open her drawers you will very oddly find there is nothing in there aside from the small, flimsy, lone paper clip and maybe one blank pink post it stuck to the side.

You get the feeling she's not a big human fan...she most assuredly has no less than 8 cats there all have some physical defect. Eye missing, three legs, tail gone, big scar going up the face. All really fun to look at.

I some cases you will have a 19 year old intern. She's very serious. She dresses in suits from Walmart and carries an attaché case for no reason whatsoever. Every time she does something good, she finds a way to get the news to the boss. What she doesn't know is he's using her to do something like data entry for 3 months the let you go. He recycles interns. She'll cry like someone told her that her dog had been run over by an SUV. She'll start slamming her drawers while she's removing the case of office supplies mom bought her.

She'll rip down pictures. Remove her little fun sticky

things on the edge of the screen of the computer. Still

sobbing hard, mind you. One younger girl whom she had

grown close to who used to be an intern and was hired,

(giving poor Walmart suit hope) will try to console her.

She'll flip out and say, "get away from me!". Then one of

the "mothers" will cut in...and poor pinstripe suit, in an

office where everyone wears jeans, will fall dramatically

into "mom's" arms. She's screaming, WHAT AM I

GONNA DO NOW?!" You're 19 years old, honey. Chances

are you'll be fine. Poor bastard. Better believe she's

running out of that office making a scene. Because

clearly she could never get a job entering data again.

I'm always a big fan of the fag, yes I said fag, who acts just flamboyant enough to be able to take a week decorating a 100 square foot office for the holiddaaaaazzzzeeee (wrist limp and parallel to the chest) it'll be done by December 22nd. So, technically you'll have one day to enjoy a very Mary Christmas...and then Suzie Q will take 2 weeks to take them down and "sssssssort them accordingly because I posssitively reFFFussse to go through this catasssstrophe next year." So, here's Sabrina, huffing and puffing like a sissy, carefully placing plastic angel figurines wrapped in papyrus paper going into the tough bins his sugar daddy provided. At the end of the week, Margo will have to request a mental health day because (s)he feels, "ugh,posssitively aawwwwful." Sitting there in the "love" on the ass  sweatpants and a very stylish teal green hoodie....and girls listen. If you have tight sweatpants that say "Juicy" on the ass, expect people to look so sucking your teeth at some guy you made a comment about your ass because you have a sparkly JUICY right on it. 90 year old women are inappropriately ogling you. He may go as far as to wear designer sandals with very fancy socks. Ps: I don't give a shit if anyone is offended so don't waste your breath. Every gay male I've ever had is reading this out loud at their regular monthly brunch that started at 4 for fashion reasons, drinking the most expensive martinis out of glorious goblets, on the floor, very dramatically laughing. They would find you "absolutely dreadful"

.....and last but not least...there is always one person who you're completely attached to. They're more of a spouse than your spouse. This is the person you feel lost without when they call in sick to work. And you proceed to email and text all day long.

And yes, every workplace says, "we should make a sitcom about this office."

If, poor thing, you work completely alone, you'll have to run around all day covering these bases. Good luck and go with God.

Ps: no matter how hot, no matter how tempting, no matter how much overtime your spouse believes you're actually working.....DO NOT SHIT WHERE YOU EAT....DO NOT SHIT WHERE YOU EAT....DO NOT SHIT WHERE YOU EAT...who came up with such a despicable cliché? ick...but just in case you didn't hear me before, you stubborn asshole...do NOT shit where you eat. Because, guess what, you're not fooling a single soul. You're about as discreet as a cowboy names Billy Jo, walking through Harlem yelling YEEEEEEEHAW! Very very big, very very foolish. If you open and run a business together. If your partner there is a supervisor who has the power to promote you and they do, then obviously it's not based on merit. It's based on what you're capable of under the duvet. Listen, we have enough to worry about as it is. Try working side by side you're not out with and tell me that their overcompensation of making sure nobody thinks anything so they start flirtatiously rubbing some gross man/woman's arm, doesn't make you want to move their desk out into traffic. Listen, if you're out as a couple, that's an entirely different thing. However, if you bring your home into work, at least you'll have a partner go with you to get foodstamps.

**Chapter 97 and three quarters**

Weird, stupid shit I think about...and please, by all means, feel free to add your own special brand of weirdness. Google nothing. That's cheating and just no fun at all.

Where the hell did words like chair, lamp, and refrigerator come from?

I mean, is there a Mr. Cornelius <u>Sock</u> out there who was just sick and tired of having cold feet.

Ever notice in rock songs and even some line in a movie, something is always cheap? Smell of cheap wine, smell of cheap perfume, with your good bag and your cheap shoes. Cheap perfume comes up a lot. I've never really had too much exposure to cheap perfume...no NO WAIT!!! I did....I did have to deal with an imposter for about 6 months. It was when I discovered women's perfume gives me a migraine. Irony at its finest...the lesbian who gets death defying headaches from the smell of a woman.

Who went through the whole process of turning a leaf into a powder that you snort up your nose to have more energy. Or have your jaw go a mile a minute and talk nonsense to a complete stranger.

Who knew that you smoke one plant and eat another?

How many people have died from these experiments?

Who knew that tobacco was tobacco and who is tobacco? And to roll it up in some flimsy paper and spark it up? Why do we follow suit? Why would we put something that could burn is into our mouths? Why

would I bring a lighter or matches right up to my face in

order to inhale fiberglass?

*in a secret little whisper voice* (I understand

prohibition because I'm a drunk. I'd have them wheeling

in moonshine by the barrel twice a week.)

Is prostitution really "the oldest profession"? Were

women swapping oral sex for brontosaurus burgers? Did

they want first crack at the invention of fire, so they

danced topless and grunted into their John's ear?

Who is this John, anyway? Was John the first customer?

I guess that would make him the oldest consumer.

Parents...stop naming your kids John. It means that he's

a prostitute user. Unless, of course, you're comfortable

with that and maybe even enforce it. In which case, John it is. Jesus...John even means toilet. Just forget the name John. Jonathan works. Just not John.

I so want to know how the first person who sang (sung, singed) realized they were capable of that. Think some cavewoman was sitting around banging a rock on something and all of a sudden, out of nowhere, she was humming, "Stand By Me".

I notice I will heat my coffee up no less than 12 times a day...and never take a sip of it. I knew that I needed a white t-shirt this morning to go under my oh so fashionable red thermal (because that's the kind of lesbian I am). I can vaguely see that something looks possibly white at 5am, in the dark because far be it from me to walk 2 feet and turn the lamp on. Which means, naturally, that I get dressed in the dark every day.

Because I have unrealistically messy hair, no one really

bats an eye when they see me skipping down the street,

always with some kind of wild grin and overtired eyes, in

one knee high grey boot with one silver buckle on the

ankle and one slightly higher brown boot with gold

buckles going all the way up the side. Don't worry, my

ridiculous lip ring always gets me through the door.

Nobody wants to mess with an almost middle aged

woman with a snug fish hook gripping her lip. I can't

remove this delightful piece of jewelry without a

blowtorch and some heavily tattooed man named Kevin

who doesn't speak. Don't ask. The white t-shirt I picked

has what seems to be a wine bottle with a tag attached

that reads "drink me". Think maybe I bought that while I

was drunk? No, I'm really asking because I could have

been in the throes of a blackout so if there were any witnesses, please feel free to drop me a line.

What man discovered that tying a piece of cloth around your neck made you look dressed up? (that would be a neck or bowtie)

There's a snippet of what runs through my head in 10 minutes. Clearly why a book I write has no real order or direction. You basically get a different me in every chapter. Half the time I'm even confused so don't worry.

**Friends….they come in all shapes and attitudes**

John Kennedy once said, "forgive your enemies but, never forget their names (check this quote) I've come to realize that our worst enemies were at some point or another, our closest friends. This isn't some genius reality. It's actually pretty obvious. Few things in life are more painful than someone pulling the shit out of the back of your emotion closet for all the world to see. You've been close enough to this person to have told them your innermost creepiness and guess what? One day that creepiness is going to be broadcast in your hometown. It's very sad when you get to an age where you really know beyond a shadow of a doubt that trusting people does not come easily. In the long run, if you have a little handful or even one for that matter, friends who you can trust, who trust you, who you can depend on for a laugh in a crisis, who vaults your innermost psychosis, then you're very lucky.

You could have that loud Italian friend who yells in place of her "inside" voice and generally drops F bombs more often than she's probably aware of. She married a nice Italian boy and they have 2 nice Italian children....and all of their volume is up to 100. This friend will kill anyone who hurts you so you have t be careful complaining about your significant other to them. You could have a totally reconcilable argument with your partner but, for now, you wanna vent about something very simple like what a prick they are for buying that slut a shot ....you have just told this outrageously protective friend and she translates that into your partner cheats on you relentlessly, blows through money we don't have, probably got an STD from the hooker s/he bought the shot for...and naturally .."WHAT IS THIS SHIT ALCOHOLIC DOING DRINKING FUCKINNNNNN' IN FRONNA YOU?! ARE YOU FUCKINNNNNN' SERIOUS?! FUCKINNNNN' IDIOT! I'll KILL'em, Sar...I'll FUCCKKINNNNNN' KILL THAT RAT BASTIT (that's bastard in Staten Island). As she violently waves a homemade sauce (yes, we call it gravy...not sauce...even though my belief is that gravy is the brown deliciousness that could turn any train wreck of a meal you tried to concoct. Burn it? Drown it in gravy. Drop it on the floor...dust it off. Drown it in gravy. Know that the meat is at least a year expired? Gravy will do the trick! Trying to hide that it's leftover chicken from 2 days ago? Whip up some instant stuffing, throw it in the pot...bathe it in gravy and voila! You now have

Thanksgiving surprise in July! And all of that was to explain what's splattering off of her wooden spoon...man. Circus music, easily. Cut my head open and out will shoot Entrance of the Gladiators...fun fact. That's what the circus music is called. I'm thinking when the Gladiators were trying to make they're masculine grand entrance in basically a metal tank top and underwear, they weren't banking on it also being the introduction to clowns throwing buckets of confetti on people. Even after we all know its confetti in the bucket, we still flinch like maniacs....yep, off track again.) Anyhoo...now your friend will argue with her husband telling me I need to come live with them to be safe from the volatile pimp I'm involved with. In the case of this friend...whenever someone confronts you, unless you want that person incapacitated, watch what you say and how you say it.

Which leads me to overprotective friend #2.... I will explain later why I have so many overprotective friends...I mean, yes. You can come to your own conclusion that I'm a hot mess and need constant supervision but, it goes deeper than that.

So, second friend (now the only reason I use nationalities is because I'd rather give you a visual reference. You'd be full of shit if you say I'm profiling because we all now damn well that different nationalities produce personalities.) friend number 2 is someone who laughs at absolutely everything. She's the kind of friend you can be around and know it'll never get too serious and if it does we'll comfort each other and then find a way to make fun of it. Defense mechanism much? Nnaahhhhh. Easily one of the most beautiful women alive aesthetically and never shows anything but being just as beautiful on the inside. Now here we have a girl who could be wearing a dainty sundress and spikes...not heels...spikes....with her finger waving in your face as her head bobs telling you, if you hurt me, that she only has to make one phone call and you are "FUCKIN' DONE!!! ONE FUCKIN' PHONE CALL!!!" Now, I've been friends with this woman for 24 years...I still don't know who that phone call is but, I would imagine it's not a pretty phone call. I always wonder if it's saved in her phone as "the one phone call." We became very close after one day she slid me a letter in chemistry that said she had lost her virginity...and I very smoothly

shouted out loud, "WOW!!!" Right in the middle of a

pretty important lesson. Needless to say, I was the

partner who was never allowed to touch the Bunsen

burner. And even if we were just talking, I was always

required to wear goggles. I wasn't very good at anything

scientific.


Now...we have the friend who is ferociously loyal. She's

the one who says things that are brash and offensive

and utterly and completely right. She's ridiculously

brilliant yet remains so perfectly down to earth. On our

first meeting, she made it somewhat clear that she was

having a "curiosity" moment. On that same meeting she

announced that she was happy she wasn't attracted to

me. Mmhhhmmm....and all that did....was bring us closer. I certainly felt like I must have looked like the hunchback of Notre Dame that night. Fact is, after that one night, I knew I made a brutally honest friend. BRUTALLY honest. Now, trust me when I tell you, all of my friends are straight and all of them are painfully beautiful. Very cute for a single lesbian who wants to post her engagement picture in the local paper. I wonder if I do this to torture myself. Anyway, this is the friend who you say, "get a shovel and some tarp" and she'll get in the car and tell you she brought 3 different sized tarp and an ice pick just in case the ground is too hard. And never once ask what it is that we're doing. Maybe she's that "one phone call".

Then there's the friend who you absolutely call to tell you're breathing, you're peeing, you're buying a birthday card, you just locked the car door, your hand moved...you know that friend. This friend really does double over 42 miles away when you get a stomach ache. This friend loves when you call her an asshole because she made you laugh that hard. She's the one whose car pulls up in front of your house because your voice sounded funny. She's the one you automatically make a copy of your front door key for. She's one who takes your shit because she knows it's not about her. She's the one who will interrupt your sentence to say, "I love you." because you made her happy. She doesn't ask what you want to drink when she runs into the store, because she already knows. She puts your happiness before hers because when you're happy, she's happy. It works out ok because you do the same for her so in

essence, you're both so happy you should be locked up.

This is the one person on earth you'd be perfectly ok

stranded on an island with and would be a little annoyed

when the Coast Guard found you. She tells you things

she wouldn't even consider telling anyone else and

when you're around, the world just seems a little

funnier. This is the face of the person who you'll expect

to see turn the corner when they're snapping the

bracelet on you in the emergency room because she's

the one you list as your emergency contact on every

form you've ever filled out. If you miss a day, scratch

that, if you miss an hour speaking, you forget what your

name is and feel like you're having an asthma attack.

...it just feels really important to me to say....you know you meet good people when you're in grammar school and a teenager. But you're a child and then a teenager, so you're a ninny. I've had the same best friends for 23 years...so I'm blessed that I wasn't that much of a ninny. As an adult, I have to say, I have never gotten more support, better compliments and just a generally good sense of self than from the people I met when I was anywhere from 3 until 14. I look at your beautiful families, your beautiful spouses...I see happiness. Well, I see pictures. Who knows what goes on behind all of our doors? But you've encouraged me in strange and beautiful ways...and I know you can't possibly know that because I never say it. I'm sorry for that. Know that I think you're the most beautiful people I know...and to know you all again now, is truly a gift. With my heart, I wish all of you happiness, laughter, passion, health and most of all.....love. You're angels on earth...my angels. More than you know. Humbly...I thank you all!

I have the kind of friends you wish for. I have the kind of friends who make me happy that I'm alive.

There's always one friend who always curses at really inappropriate times

Always one who you relentlessly talk about sex to.

There's one friend who can absolutely read your mind

And one you'd easily name as godparent of your child

There's only one you can sit in comfortable silence with

And one who never stops talking ever

There's one who is eternally looking for love so she

latches on to anyone who calls her a term of

endearment.

There is one who lies for really no apparent reason

And there's that one poor bastard who always gets stuck at the table everywhere you go to watch the purses and coats.

There's one who hasn't quite reached her peak yet so watch out when she does because she's going to be fierce

There's one who will always tell you look beautiful even when you look like shit

And the one who's close enough to you...to tell you that you look like shit

There's one friend who always seems to have weird

symptoms she wants to explain to you



She's the one who's smart enough to realize that you

have no idea what the name of the person is that you're

speaking to so without even a second to waste, she'll

jump in and introduce herself so you can get the name

of this person who is talking to you like you've known

them for 100 years.



And one that will always go see horror movies with you

There's the one who drags you to movies she knows you hate...be she goes to see the horror movies with you so you're shit out of luck

There's always one friend who gets an obnoxious amount of attention everywhere you go

And one who's just downright obnoxious but you love her anyway

There's one you know is a lesbian so she overcompensated by constantly talking about penis

There's one who will get drunk and try to hit on your

spouse...watch out for her

Then there's always one who just gets drunk too damn

much

You may have a closet drug addict in your clan. Watch

for orange bottles in her bag, incessant gum chewing, or

long sleeves in the summer time.

There's always one who always looks good in a bathing

suit yet eats 5 cheeseburgers and 6 hotdogs at every

damn BBQ you go to.

There's always a mother hen

There's going to be a few who will go absolutely ape shit if someone does something to you

There's always one friend who speaks another language and she's never there when someone speaks to you in that language.

There's a gold digger...

And one, who just works her ass off, has perfect credit and every bill is paid the day before it's due. She probably hasn't had sex in a long time so be careful what you say to her sometimes. She's probably pretty edgy.

There's one who absolutely hates her husband's guys

and finds him repulsive yet never leaves him


There's one who will all but carry her child around until

they're 43 and one who would let their 2 year old scale a

building during a hail storm (she might be the one with

the prescription bottle in her bag, so watch her)


One who just cooks phenomenally without effort


And one who is and has been on every diet known to

man and can't lose a pound

And one who eats a pint of chubby hubby a night and

never gains one


One who shops way too much


And one who waits until 2 hours before a function to ask

if she can borrow something of yours


One wears lipstick no matter what she's doing ....and

one that just flat out wears too much damn makeup.


There's one that hates your spouse...hates them!

There's one that is envious of you

There is one who could crawl into bed next to you and watch TV laying your arm and neither one of you would flinch from discomfort.

One is a pig. I'm sorry but it's true...one of you is a whore and you know it.

One always seems to keep a friendship with one of your exes even if it bothers you

One of them you'll love with all of your heart and slowly

lose contact with - don't worry, she'll pop up again

There's one that makes you laugh hard enough to have

to keep yelling, "STOP STOP STOP STOP!" To while

holding your stomach and waving

One of them always knows the perfect time to look up at

you.

One of them you fight with far too often and make up

with always.

One is going to betray you if she hasn't already.

There's one you'd rather talk to than text any day of the week.

And one whose call you won't answer because you'd rather text.

There's one who will make you drop your perishable groceries on the ground and bolt out the door if you so much as hear her voice crack.

One of them posts really inappropriate things on your Facebook page and either thinks it's funny or does it just to bust your balls.

One of them is really not your friend

That poor bastard who gets stuck watching the coats and bags....she'll have someone fall in love with her. Head over heels and she'll be the one who lives the life we only dream about.

One just has too many damn kids - and at least one of those children is so rotten you fantasize about locking him in the closet.

One jerk continuously puts you on the phone with new boyfriends/girlfriends to "get to know each other" and God forbid you actually do get along and maybe start talking somewhat regularly, she'll get mad and start ignoring you.

If a friend is one word answering you, she is really pissed off at you. If you care about this girl, I recommend finding out why.

If a friend asks you if something's bothering you, don't disgustedly huff at her...it means she cares about you and what's to be there for you....and she probably knows that getting something out of you is like trying to pull the molar out of a very hungry lion.

One friend's dog jumps all over you and maybe every so often she'll say, "Mittens (the name of her Pit bull/Rottweiler mix....and I am a pit bull fan, pit bull lovers. My description is based on size and strength. (Funny, I worry more about insulting dogs than people. I think that's fair to say with most human beings) she'll whisper, "Mittens...get ddooooowwwnnnn....hey ppssstttttt pssstttt...come here...Mmmiittteeeennnnnsssssss come to mmommmyyyyyy..." Mittens will have a death grip on you femoral artery and would have been humping you now for a steady 9 minutes. She wonders why you don't come over more to visit and will actually say, "Mittens

misses her Aauunnnttt Ssaaarrrraaaaahhhhh....*high

pitched* don't you Mittens YeaH YeaH you miss your

Aunt Sawwaahhhhh...RIGHT?! Ooh such a good

ggiirrrlllllll..." That shit will go on for a good 5 minutes -

and you know, no matter how many times she tells

Mittens to tell you she misses you, 9 times out of 10,

Mittens won't and the one time she does, call 911 and

take a much needed rest.


One friend will not wash her hair for 5 days because

some hair dresser told her it's not healthy to wash your

hair every day. What the hair dresser forgets to say is it

is unhealthy for everyone around you to be subjected to

that dirty scalp smell - if you have too much hair...then

either get up early enough to scrub your scalp or shave

your head. Dirty scalp smell is right up there with that

nubby thing you bite into in cheap hamburgers and that

weird fatty tip you'll always find inside of a chicken leg.


One friend constantly walks out of your house with one

of your favorite sweaters or sweatshirts and positively

never returns them. She'll think nothing of wearing it

out when she's hanging out with you too. Better believe

there is now a ketchup stain in the dead center that will

never come out. That's when she'll give it back to you

and feverishly claim it was there when she borrowed it

from you in 1987.

I was the girl who watched the bags and jackets....and no, I haven't quite met my match, well, I have met my match, she just didn't get the memo yet on loving me back. Mutter, "her loss" to me one time, and I will remove your kneecaps. I've heard it 14 billion times and my guess is she's not feeling the winded chest pains I get if I allow myself to think of her for even a millisecond. Better to have loved and lost??? Um, no. I say better to have never had those moments in public when you have to grab your mouth or pinch so hard between your eyes to keep from bursting into tears at any given moment even when it's unprovoked. PASS thank you! When your chin suddenly looks like you held a cheese grater against it for an hour and half and you get those weird little wrinkly bumps from pursing your lips far too hard, you're not fooling anyone and someone will always see it and generally say, "OH MY GOD! ARE YOU ALRIGHT?!"

And you will never be able to verbally answer that question unless you feel like hollering (I don't mean just crying. I mean flat out hollering) in a very public place. My advice is, if the tears start coming up when you're alone, meet them out while you can. You never want a client to be the one who's rubbing your back telling you "everything's gonna be okkkkkk....it's her llooosssssssssss..." (Longest description of friend I've given so far. Think I'm a little bitter?")

There is one friend you will say mean things to - too mean to even be fixed and you will regret that for the rest of your life. The lesson is, be mindful of someone else's feelings and watch what you say to your best friend. No one is made of steel and not everything can "be ok". When we say, "you always hurt the ones you love." It's a damn shame that it's true.

You'll make a friend in life that will open up to you in ways that will change your views on things forever.

Somebody please at least buy a beer for that poor girl at the table with the coats and bags. Or, as the case may be, a ginger ale.

One of your friends wears flip flops all year round

One will always have baby wipes in her bag...and baby wipes do EVERYTHING. Clean your hands, your peepees, a blood stain, cures colds...tells you everything is going to be ok. Baby wipes are God's way of saying, "thank you"

There is one who can have one drink in a four hour night and be perfectly ok with that. She doesn't have a license so you're fucked anyway.

One of your friend gets psycho jealous when she sees you refer to another friend as your best and gets equally serial killer-ish when she sees you post an "I love you" on someone else's Facebook page. Your phone will also ring the very instant you say "thank you" to someone because she positively needs to know why. Appease her or she will eventually feel like she has to kill you in order to be "free again" - the last words you'll hear, "See what you made me do!"

One friends laugh instantly makes you laugh even when you don't know what she's laughing at and one friends laugh will go straight up your spine like glass.

One friend misses you, wants to call you but is afraid you won't want to hear from her. She does....call her.

One friend has her damn Christmas cards sent by November 18th and her shopping done in October.

....and hopefully there is one friend or maybe even more...that is really just your family. She could just as soon be your twin...or he...I keep leaving the guys out of this...guys, I'm sorry. That person who you can't live without....and who can't live without you. Several people will come in and out unfortunately but, in the end, there will be that one who can read your mind. Who not only finishes your sentences but can say them for you. Who wouldn't dream of letting anything or anyone come between you. Someone you trust without even the slightest hesitation. In that persons "boat of life" if there are 5 people in their boat and one of them has to go in order to save the rest, you don't even blink because you know you're not one of those 5. They would just as soon throw themselves into that water to make sure you were safe. So, that being said, if you have that one person....call them up right now and tell them you love them and thank them for always being there for you. Never take for granted that one person is a warrior in your life. Let them know it.

As a matter of fact....take a day and tell every one of those friends you love them because they're perfect just the way they are. Tell them that in your eyes, they're perfect.

**Extraordinary Woman**

I'm very lucky to have been chosen to be a part of the company I work for. I had attended school and graduated from The Resource Training Center/ Recovery and Life Coaching Academy. Easily one of the most highly influential, successful companies in the field of rehabilitation. The company is owned and operated by Donna Mae Depola (Twelve Tins) highly recommended, very intense autobiography and her partner Dona Pagan partner in life, partner in business, partner in crime and truly are each other's biggest fans. They met in their 50's so I figure I have another 12, 13 years left for Mrs. Right...or Mrs. You'll have to do because I'm getting too old to be picky and I'm tired of eating dinner alone. The staff at this brilliant company is made up of a festival of colorful people....I mean, let's face it, I know I've been in a psych ward at least 4 times and one of them was in the seriously dangerous part of that ward where they had bars on top of bars and refused to give me a pencil. Tough to do a crossword puzzle with half of a paperless red crayon. It was either that or watch Vera (true story) sit with her leg over the arm of a dialysis chair with no underclothes, slapping, yes slapping her, uh, private parts yelling toward me, thinking I was someone named Henry, who was obviously very bad to her. You never want to remind an elderly, under-pantless woman that you remind her of someone named Henry who she clearly dislikes. I decided to grow my hair out a bit and walk around topless but I suppose Henry had C cup man boobs. See, that's the fun part, you can walk around completely topless and scream JIMMY CRACK CORN AND I DOONNN'T CCAAARRRREEEEE....and no one would bat an eye. If you're somewhat normal or at least have some faculties left, you realize how fantastic your life is and to stop being a whiny bastard about how awful your life is on the other side of that gate. For instance (now this is a true story...not some rendition just to get your attention. All psych ward stories are positively true) the young Hispanic boy. Maybe no more than 19 years old, sitting beside me in the "community lounge" (nothing in a psych ward should be named lounge. It's ridiculous.) looks at me and says, "do you like clowns?" See now, that in of itself is creepy enough. Do I just say no and pretend like I just went into crazy stare land? Nope. I sure don't. I say, "yeah, I like clowns." (I didn't elaborate and tell him my dream was to go to clown college because who knows if he hates clowns and I'm about to get my ass handed to me for just saying yes). He looks straight ahead. Never once removing his gaze from something that clearly wasn't there. "I love clowns." (Again...crreeeeeeeeeeeep-o) "I used to steal my mother's make-up and paint clown faces." Now, did clown boy mean that he drew clowns or he made himself a clown with his mom's make-up? Do I ask or am

I just lining myself up for failure? "Yeah, she used to get

real mad at me and hit me for ruining her make-up." Ok,

now I'm thinking is this kid playing weirdo with me and

playing the victim or is this very real? Now this was prior

to getting well and going into the counseling field so I'm

allowed to think negative thought about people I'm

locked behind gates with. So now I'm just staring at him

waiting for him to tell me the reason why he needed to

know if I like clowns. Is he going to be creepier by just

getting up and walking away? Is he going to tell me why

he likes them? Nope, he's going to finally turn his overly

drugged head my way and pull his left bottom eyelid

down dramatically and say, "she she she wouldn't let me

use the, uh, the make-cup...not make-up but make-cup

so I just made it where...." And clown boy most certainly

had carved clown features, like diamond shapes above and below his eye, into his face. CHECK PLEASE!!! This is where I demand to see my doctor and tell him how unbelievably normal I am and how I was just looking for attention and that I'm a drunk and just need drunk help." In the 24 hour period I had to wait for Dr. Holy Shit, I had one more young boy tell me that his landlord kicked his pregnant girlfriend down the stairs and made her miscarry so he laid in wait and when he thought the time was right, he followed his landlord into his apartment and proceeded to sodomize him with a sword. Fact is, even if he was making that up, he was still bat shit crazy enough to say it. That was when I signed a form that said NO ONE was allowed to visit me. They'd either be really upset and scared for me or scared to death that I was like this. Then I wondered, as I tried to write malodorous in dulled red crayon on the tiny crossword puzzle, am I like these people and I just don't realize because I'm as cuckoo for ...I'm not even going to make the cereal reference. It's ridiculous. I understood finally why the nurses were s nasty. I'm guessing after a while in crazyville, you'd get pretty nasty yourself. Self preserving boundaries indeed. Well, fact of the matter is sure I may not have carved a dancing poodle on my face but, I did come home from work and march right up the stairs and while still in my suit, completely shaved my head. I had an unhealthy obsession with crime shows. You should absolutely NEVER watch crime shows when you're feeling a little "off". I did become paranoid. Not to the extent that I was hearing voices or thought FBI was in the tree just waiting for their moment to strike. I just felt like people I loved were talking behind my back.

That they were whispering about me. I've filled out no less than 10 applications in my life that asked the question, "do you see shadows walking into walls?" And it wasn't until I got my life and my brain back that I realized how specific that question is. I mean, do statistics show that the majority of us unique individuals see shadows walking into walls? I never saw shadows walking into walls. Unless I did but I was too drunk to remember it. So drunk, in fact, I would have just assumed I had company and not think a thing of it. It must suck to see shadows walking into walls. Must be incredibly difficult to do some normal activities. I've heard a lot of people say they didn't want to take their meds because it didn't make them feel like themselves. Isn't that the point, chief? If someone told me that I'd have to drink a bottle of hot sauce a night with mini marshmallows you'd have to chew that had been marinating in the cup, in order to stop the shadows, bet your ass you'd be calling me Tobasco instead of Schmitty (or Sarah...whichever you feel comfortable with). They'd say they feel like a zombie. I'd take zombie any day over convincing myself that a dog owned my "Sam" was telling me to go out with a brown paper bag containing a gun that looks more like a cannon just randomly, disgustingly shooting people who were casually enjoying one another. (Son of Sam reference. And for all you young'uns...Son of Sam was a serial killer from New York.) Once I started to realize and understand that meds and treatment could give you a normal, productive life, I stopped looking at any of these people as "crazy". I began looking at them for what they are. Sick. Bottom line is, if you had any other disease, you'd treat it.

Cancer=chemo, diabetes=insulin, you'd do it. Mental illness is a treatable disease. With medication and regular doctor visits, you could make that bad boy either go into remission or never come back again. Nervous breakdowns are very real and very scary. You positively feel like what's coming out of your mouth is perfectly normal and you wonder why the person you're talking to is looking at you with fear and confusion. Your ability to differentiate fact from fiction is nil. I will tell you this...what you're feeling is very real and it can get better as long as you want it to get better. I'm not speaking as a clinician. I'm speaking as a human being who knows what it feels like to lose touch with reality. I positively know that when you're having an anxiety attack, it feels very much like you're having a heart attack. It does pass and yes, sometimes you do need a professional to get you through it. Anxiety is a healthy human reaction. It's what keeps us from wondering into the street when a bus is coming. Surely you must have a tiny bit of anxiety about that bus potentially rolling over you. Do some house cleaning too. Surrounding yourself with negative people will only have me outcome. And you can't save them, my little codependent friend. They're gonna have to save themselves. Along with Alcohol Induced Psychosis which is relatively self explanatory. I also have a very distinct case of PTSD (Post Traumatic Stress Disorder) that I left unattended starting with the day I stood under the South Tower of the World Trade Center and watched a plane so low and so close that it literally broke the sound barrier, fly through the building with as much obvious purpose to me, I was never the same. From that day forward, everything that I had known about who I was and how I felt, died that day. I spoke about the experience to close friends and family just briefly after it had happened and then threw it in the back of a dingy old closet and never took a look at it again. Now, where you would think a life altering, life threatening event like 9/11 would make me cherish life, it instead turned me into an angry, risk taking ninny who was very difficult to be around. I haven't decided yet if I want to tell the whole story of that day, yet. It may come up...it may not. I can go from being a lot of fun and very relaxing to be around to a very frightening, very cold, very arrogant person. One day you could say, "hey Sarah! How are you?" and I'll answer you easily with, "I'm doing ok! How are you?". The very next day you could say, "hey Sarah! How are you?" And I will also easily respond, "WHAT THE FUCK

DO YOU MEAN, HOW AM I !? You know EXACTLY how I am!! Fucking RIDICULOUS! How the fuck AM I !? HOW THE FUCK ARE YOU !?" Alcohol Induced Psychosis. Most of the times I drank, I blacked out. I would go for 5 or 6 hours completely mentally unconscious, yet physically awake and communicative. Not much of what in had said made much sense. If I had done something particularly stupid that was grounds to lose one or many friends, I would be able to flip on the water works and scream ridiculous things like, "I HAVE PROSTATE CANCER!!! No one even knows I'm a man, and now I have testicular, prostate, foreskin cancer!!! I don't know how to deal with the loss. I'm not acting out...I'm scared! I'm scared of losing my friends because none of you knew I was a man and now I'm at risk of losing my penis!!!" Yep. I surely would say things that ridiculous and get crazy angry if you tried to tell me I can't possibly have prostate cancer and I don't really have a penis. Even smoother even I'm yelling this at someone who is currently or once was a lover (cornball word).

So, the day the doctor told me that I was free to leave. I was in normal shape and not a danger to myself and society. Why was I in the in the first place? Well, I have something called Alcohol Induced Psychosis which pretty much speaks for itself I have extreme Jekyll & Hyde syndrome. Any time I ever woke up in a hospital, I had no idea why and had to depend on the word of people who are really pissed off at me. So, the instant I walked out of that crazy prison and said goodbye to all of my fun friends and politely asked Vera if she could be a lamb and put her vagina away before I open the door. There was no way I was saying goodbye to Vera less than 10 feet away. I watched as my little man made harlequin looked on sadly and before I make a funny comment as a blatant defense mechanism, I wonder if his family has just dubbed him "crazy" and just abandoned him. I wonder if sword guy is really telling the truth and if so, is his girlfriend pleased with, what he thought, was an act of chivalry. And then I also wonder if none of that is real. No girlfriends, no baby, no landlord, no sword. Vera, well dear Vera, I believe is a little too far into her world that she'll never be able to really come back again. Having heard her rants basically 24/7, I was given the impression that her husband (Henry) brutalized her and let his friends brutalize her as well. Now, Vera's about 75 years old so in a time when she was being assaulted by all of these men, I'm sure the women just looked at her like she was a whore. Not like she was in danger...rather just a hussy. It really aggravated the shit out of me that I reminded her of her husband. I know that my actions didn't warrant that. My guess is Henry looked like a lesbian.

So as the years went on, I wondered if maybe I had allowed her to believe that I was her husband and behaved kindly to her maybe she would have had some closure. Granted, I'm not a mental health professional but I am human. I wonder if I could have opened the door to the cage she was in by feigning an apology from someone who was very obviously an asshole. But the whole slapping herself thing is really a major deterrent.

What would have happened if I did get close to offer some peace and before I could react, she touches me? The feeling of grossness would have washed over me enough to have caused a heart attack.

Lest I forget, silly me. In the psych ward (or at least my psych ward) you have your own room with a bathroom connecting you to the other patient's bed. Needless to say, while taking a shower, instead of flip flops, I wore snow tires. I had no doubt that I was sharing my bathroom with someone whom needed to be watched while shaving. Over her hospital gown, she wore a man's blazer (tweed with the suede patches on the elbow... In case you needed a visual) a trucker cap that is just paced on top of her head with a completely flat, untouched brim. She wore glasses that were maybe a centimeter below those novelty oversized glasses. She would pace up and down the hall yelling stuff in Spanish. Well, needless to say, she would lock the door preventing me from using the bathroom. S, no less than 4 times a day, I had to have staff unlock the door and give her an adult timeout. Every time she came out of adult timeout, that bastard would lock my door again. Well, one night I decided I was going to give her a run for her money. I locked her door. *sigh* I will never lock the door of someone who wears a blazer over a backless hospital gown, trucker cap and novelty sunglasses...again. I heard the first handle jiggle and did that little giggle into the hand bit. Then I heard the jiggling pick up speed. She was jiggling with vim and vigor, if you will. Now came the long hard jiggle. Where she seems like she's trying to snap it loose. Now, we have banging. I'm not giggling into my hand. I'm looking straight up at the water stained ceiling thinking, "fffffuuuuuccckkkk....they're so gone know that I did this on purpose. This might have bought me another day in la la land. 10 seconds of silence....and this earth shattering shrill like someone was stabbing her came through the door. Now, here she is screaming on the top of her lungs. Remember now, she's speaking Spanish. Now while I know shouting in a different language always makes someone understand better, not one word did I get from her. I'm listening to this awful shrieking and wondering, "Jesus, how much louder and creepier does this woman need to yell?! It's not like we're on lockdown in here. Who's to say that sword boy or his friend Bozo didn't make their way down the corridor with their imaginary night vision goggles? So now it's time to make my move. I'll book to the bathroom, unlock her door and book back to my blue plastic foam mattress that is oh so comfortable and definitely helps with sleepless nights and anxiety.

1......2......3.....RUN....as I'm stuck in crane like stance, the orderly runs into my room and in that state of panic I begin to act out the black swan's role from Swan Lake. Another fantastic thing in the psych ward. You can positively get away with the madness of performing a ballet in your pitch black room in the middle of the night. As far as they're concerned, you're incorporating healthy habits...like ballet. Even if I have a shaved head and a football jersey, being known universally as Henry. Ballet looked very natural for me. Especially when I did that creepy, exaggerated run in a wide circle. All this time, mind you, gorgeous on the other side of the bathroom door is still screeching. Now I'm torn between my feigned craziness and my reality that I must have triggered something awful for this woman. Finally they realize they can save themselves a whole lotta trouble by coming into my special rendition of this very famous ballet and unlocking the bathroom door from my side. Geniuses. Well, yes, they had to sedate her to calm down. So, what do I do next? Better believe I start screaming my head off so I can have a shot too. That's the mind of a drug addict. I would make up ailments like collaborative chin disintegration that was causing me a lot of pain and tell them that I normally take morphine for it but since I'm here and I want to follow the rules, I'll settle for Percocet. How often do I take it? 4 times an hour. I take two four times an hour. Now, if they don't give me 2 four times a day, I can't act like a maniac because of the pain I'm really not in which will make them just do anything you ask. Better to have a mellow house then to have Henry wind everybody up.

Sadly, I knew that I wasn't on the same level as the other patients because what I had was brought on by liquor. If I wasn't drinking, everyone was safe. The reason I say sadly is because I couldn't imagine having gotten so lost along the way that I'd have resigned myself to live in a place where meals become weapons of mass destruction. That I knew, before it was too late, that I really didn't belong there. Sadly, it didn't "scare me straight". I continued to drink myself into psychosis and really in the end...it was almost the end. Sometimes I wonder if those people are still behind metal gates or if they've gotten the right kind of help they needed in order to live a fairly normal life. I'm wondering if whatever made the guitar string in their head break (because, for me, it sounded like that when I finally snapped), they finally got some peace with. I'm thinking Vera's resting in some kind of peace. Can't be worse than the hell she was probably in on this earth. Clown boy was very young. I'm hoping he just has faint scars that no one would recognize if they didn't know him when I did. Sword fella, if he did do what he said he did, is still behind the steel that separates him from us.

I didn't get the help I needed for many years. 7, I would say. 7 years of living inside of a crowded head is just too damn long. Problem is, you really don't know when it's a problem until you recognize someone tilting there head and scrinching their eyebrows at you while you're talking. If their mouth is a little bit open, you're a mess and better get yourself to a doctor aaayyyyy esssssssss aayyyyyyy peeeeeeeee! Yes, I do take medication. Nothing over the top. It's not even an antidepressant of anti anxiety....it's anti seizure. The latest trend. Regardless of what it is, few (not all) people look at me like the dog who's hearing "wanna go for a WALK?! You wanna go for a WALK?! WALK?! Yeah?!" And although I don't have a therapist, I work in a field with people who were just as unique and interesting as I was and there really is strength in numbers. Normally if I was writing this book and I was a receptionist at a doctor's office, I'm pretty sure they'd find some obscure reason to fire me the week after the book launched. What a truly lucky girl

I am. I can be myself in all aspects. I highly recommend it.

**Quick thought:**

I have a pretty good handle on addiction and what it's about. I'm fairly well versed in the disease, how it works and how to at least begin or try to begin working toward a pathway to wellness.

I'm fairly sure, although I haven't been trained in this particular topic that sex addiction is or has to be somewhat similar to any other.

But is really a smart idea to have meetings? I don't know...and trust me at some point I will learn and correct myself. This is only a thought. See, I'm a pill addict and a booze addict so, if to my right was a bottle of Roxicet and to my left was, I don't know, say, a beer (I was never partial to any one liquor, I just tossed it back no matter how ferocious) during my meeting, I might have a tough time, um, focusing. Not present day but, when I was first getting sober, yes.

That being said. If I am addicted to sex and I'm sitting between two sex addicts, looking across the room at more sex addicts while talking about sex....I would probably have a tough time heading home alone that night. Hell, I would just as soon probably walk in a sleeping bag and no pants.

Just a thought.

## God's gift to Schmitty

In absolute darkness, I prayed. In the full blown light, I prayed. I prayed when I didn't even know I was praying. I asked for the strength to give the gift of strength....because even at my worst, I knew I was worthy of God's love. I knew, because they told me in religion class that God gives special talents. Today God held up a big neon sign that read, "Your ready....YOUR MOMENT IS RIGHT NOW!" Through my sickness and my scars...through scabs of bad decisions and horrible moments of impulsive hate, I broke free. Today I was given permission to give my strength away. I was allowed to see what God had given me. He gave me the love, the knowledge, the patience, the strength and the peace of mind to pull one of His children out of darkness and pull her into my light. Today is the day I became the woman I silently begged to be. Today I became someone I never thought I deserved to be. I felt a wave of peace come over me that I have never known...and I cried. I didn't stop myself...I just let it go...and then I danced. True story...I danced and I sang while I cleaned up my office. Imagine...MY OFFICE!!! Two years ago, I begged to make sure that when I fell asleep, I just wouldn't wake up because I was too drunk to get out of my bed. That bed...my prison that I absolutely refuse to sleep in today. Today God gave me wings and told me, "Sarah, it's your day to fly!" And I took a deep breath, I gave

every ounce of my faith that He wouldn't let me

fall....spread those beautiful wings...and I soared. Lord,

you've given me the gift of saving your children from

darkness. I will cherish this gift and I will give it lovingly.

And I thank you....thank you God....for ALWAYS believing

in me. Thank you for never granting me the wish of not

seeing another day because every day I open my eyes, I

am truly grateful. So to you, my friend, my God I say

AAAAAAAMMMMMMMEEEEEEENNNNNNNNN!!!!!



Listen to me....YOU are NEVER too old to absolutely

jump off the path you're on. Never waste a single

second of your life on a path that's loaded with

potholes. Make sure your path has its healthy obstacles

so you remember to stay humble. This life....this one

thing...is yours alone. If you don't love, trust and

appreciate you...you'll always be walking on someone

else's path. My dear friend, it is never too late to decide

you want your own path....because you're stronger than

you know. Trust me.

## The Storm After the Calm

.....Amen to the next morning where the adrenalin has

left itself on the decorative couch pillow I passed my

bowling ball head out on last night. I don't remember if

I've ever slept like that, so that's cool. You know you're

tired when you fall asleep on a decorative pillow. It's like

waking up in sandpaper and faux-velvet. Which would

make me question why I have anything velveteen for

decoration purposes and wonder if I'm ever going to feel

like joining 2013. I'm getting ready this morning and I

have wrinkles. Yep, I sure do. Wrinkles and dark, dark

like I've been punched in the face dark rings under my

eyes. I have earned my stripes. I don't know if I feel

nauseous or exhilarated. Or nauseous from being

exhilarated. Definitely not exhilarated because I'm

nauseous. That's a definite. My voice has changed...not

tremendously but for you old timers out there, I sound a

little like Brenda Vaccaro for you new timers I can only

think of Lindsay Lohan at the moment. After she's been

punched in the throat...or smoked 2 packs of cigarettes.

I've been smoking one of those fancy new electric

cigarettes which are fabulous because I'm a self loathing

smoker. I can't stand the smell, the taste, the invasion of

other people's personal space because I'm smoking. So,

here's this great new invention that allows me to carry

around this questionable mechanism that I secretly

bring up to my mouth in inappropriate places and really

believe no one knows what I'm doing. I bought a pink,

yes they have pink, one thinking that might throw them

off. But what the hell pink and green broken pen like

looking thing that blazes orange at the end seems

acceptable in a doctor's office? How do I hide the cloud

of smoke it allows you to blow out? I hold it in. Smart

right? Do I question what this superb vapor is? I sure

don't. Do I wonder what it is that's inside of this little

miracle that allows me to blow rings out of my mouth

and only at the very last second realize that no, my 5

year old nephew should not try it. I remember my boss saying, "no, I won't use it because there are no long term studies on it yet." Ok, well, there are long-term studies on actual cigarettes and from the TV commercial these days; people are losing fingers over it. Do I believe this little friend I have now is ultimately safe? Um, well, I carry it around like a pacifier and have been known to walk a mile back home to retrieve it. So, as I sit here on the ferry with my pacifier in my lap, I'll look around coolly to see if anyone is watching me...and then I'll pull this mystery smoke up to my mouth and realize....there is positively no point to this. But does there really always need to be? And I don't mean that to sound like a depth question. I mean, truly, does the mind really always need to have a point or can't we just.....well...can't we just?

## Snappy looker

I'm one of those slick characters who, for one reason or another, will walk around Herald Square, chin up, goofy grin...a little bit of swagger....And my zipper alllllllll the wwwaayyyyy down!

More people have seen the front of my underwear than people who I'm intimate with who I'm actually removing my underwear for. Which is good because if the amount of people I've slept with is comparable to midtown NY, then we need to talk.

I'm the kind of girl with short hair who must terminally look like bed head because I have 6 cow licks. (Cow lick....what a gross analogy....cow liked me so much, she dragged her hock of a tongue all over my head)I leave the house knowing the back of my hair is standing straight up and you'd believe I still think I'm cool. If you ever see me with flat hair, I'm either sick or I just cheated on you. I generally lean toward "yyeeaahhh...I'm just not feeling too good." My hair had once been described as "a 7 year old boy on picture day who doesn't know how to comb his hair." That was a good, long, uncomfortable silence...*crickets*..."So my hair looks awful?" "No! I love it!" Lately I've been having menopausal hot flashes. Let me explain something to you, and yes I know you're saying, "but you're too yoouunnggg, pick pick pick..!" I'm the same age my mother was, sorry mom, so cool it. Hot flashes will wake you up in the middle of the night convinced the house is on fire. Hot flashes will make you walk down the street in a bra and your pants open and look furiously at people as you try to juggle the winter clothes you thought you would have need. Change flying out of every pocket, coat sleeve dragging on the ground, easily considering throwing the ridiculous turtleneck you really thought you'd survive in, right in the thrash. Could be a $750.00 cashmere sweater just dangling over the "keep our streets clean" sign. Their hair will usually be short because you just don't give a shit and the long hair dangling on your neck will only enhance the homicidal tendencies. Carrying napkins, towels, paper towels, rags, scarves, bandanas...the damn shirt off your back while fanning your hand in front of your face like that's actually gonna help. Where in actuality, fanning yourself

raises your body temperature because of your rigorous

hand movement. I'm still a little confused about drinking

hot beverages in the summer and sensitive teething the

sno-cone, while holding a death defying piece of shoddy

plastic to sled down a mountain called "Dead Man's Hill"

true story...and if you spin just enough out of control

while white knuckling the easily undoable straps, you'll

fall right into a swamp like ditch of water. If that doesn't

cure hot flashes, than I don't know what will.


Anyway, I believe I am a lot cooler than I actually am. I

also, in the very recent past, was one of those ninnies

that would wear a thin jacket in the dead of winter

because it looks cooler with the outfit. As long as I'm

sporting some silken looking scarf like an ascot and fingerless gloves, I'm all winter. I'd try to really strut and act confident, like I'm not even chilly. In actuality, I'd like to start screaming and sport that perma-scowl on my face. Nope...I'll even go as far as trying to maneuver a cigarette through a cattle drive of rush hour folks...and when I'm done...I'll professionally flick it 18 feet into the street. On some especially ridiculous day, you might even catch me lighting it with a Zippo and instead of just closing the thing with my hand, I flick my wrist as hard as I can to close it with one hand. It's amazing I have any friends who want to still be seen with me. I'm having a difficult time getting rid of the messy spike look in my hair, even though it's been out of style for a significant amount of time. It's been trained to disastrously stick up and all over. Now I don't mean spiked....I just mean a mess and up. I've been trying to retrain this hot

mess...but it's pointless. If I'm really out of control, I

have aviator sunglasses on. Now, if I've explained myself

and you can relate, then you are the same level of

douchebag I am and no one is brave enough to tell you.

No one is cool enough to dress or act this way...unless

you are a celebrity in an airport. In which case you

are...you are too obvious. Tone it down.

**Bad folks and bad intentions**

Ever notice people who relentlessly gossip are either on

the verge of divorce, severely overweight and think

nothing of ordering a platter of disco fries (for all the out

of Staten Island.....disco fries is a catering tray sized

plate of French fries soaked in the cheese of your choice

drowning in gravy) these people very masterfully

manage to get a 2 inch pile of melted cheese and a half

cup of brown gravy up to their mouth without spilling a

drop. Magnificent talent. Actually, maybe not...gossipers

are all shapes and sizes...unshowered and toothless

perhaps...outrageously beautiful but, only under their

makeup. Lots and lots of makeup. Sometimes there's an

innocent bystander that will pay the price for their

friend's mouth. It's debilitating. It's paralyzing. When

rumors start at this 40's age, it can cause the kind of

irreparable damage that could absolutely stop

someone's world. I've been accused of having an affair

with EVERY ONE of my friends...every one. Now, if their

husbands don't know me, imagine the type of horror

that could come from some asshole who never knows

when to keep their mouth shut. Shit stirrer is so textbook mediocre self esteem at best. In any event, not an ounce more of my energy with this nonsense because that's what it is...nonsense. I have always fully admitted that in some way shape or form, I have absolutely fallen head over heels in love with all of my friends. They're amazing women...and...uh...I'm a lesbian. Do I act on it...I'm thinking I might have blurted out, "yyoouuuujjzzzzzuusstttdooonnnn'ttt *deep breath in*hhooowwwwmmuuccczzhhhhiiiiiiLllllloooovvveeeyyo ouuuu...I mean I really jzussttt loveeee youu...and I wwannnnnaaaa kiiissszzyou...but I woonnn'ttt, right!? Because we we we cannnn't right? I meeaann it'szzzz entirely uupppp tooooo yyoouuuu. Because, I'm ok withhhhh thhaat." Now...that hot mess of a conversation could go on for hours. All of them appease me...kind of a pat on the head and the very deadly, very heart breaking phrase, "if I was a lesbian, you would so be my girlfriend." Yeesh....worst phrase in the world. I've had it said to me no less than 4 billion times. I don't know whether to be flattered or insulted.

These gossip folks, yes I'm giving one more second to it, should consider themselves lucky that I don't have the same disgusting disease they have. I'm relatively sure lots of divorces, lots of very violent fights and lots of lives crushed would be spread all over the table. Sshhhhhhhhhhhhhh. Start thinking before you ramble on...one day I might redeem myself by extending you the same courtesy you've extended me.

You know...I feel like going left here for a second and I'll tell you why...since you're standing in my shoes when your hand is on the page...I've explained my insomnia. Fact is I sleep terribly because my mind is always racing. But I wonder my dear friend; can you see the difference in my writing pre-recovery to post-recovery? I feel like there is just so much to tell you and chronologically I am so off, I'm only hoping you're weird and geeky enough to continue on this hurricane of a book.

I've kissed a few of my friends in high school. Truth or dare is fabulous. I'm old enough, strong enough and confident enough to be comfortable with being in love with my friends. It doesn't mean I'd cross a line but, doesn't it make perfect sense that the women I choose to bring close to me, I would feel an extreme love for.

My friends are magnificent and truly don't ever let me

down. They do what they can when they can and I

acknowledge that sometimes our lives get very busy and

it's not always easy to keep in touch. If you're that kind

of friend who needs to be up someone's ass...you are no

friend of mine. If I don't see you for 5 months...you'd

better believe when I sit down, we're gonna pick up right

where we left off.


I'll never miss the gasoline smell of coke up my nose or

in my mouth. I'll never miss waking up with cotton

mouth and a headache that appears to only be helped

with a Bloody Mary or 8 lbs of fried anything. I'll never

miss knowing that I had some intense conversation with

a complete stranger who I was convinced would be a lifelong friend....because I was fucked up out of my mind. I'll never miss ferociously eyeing up my friends who may have some left because I killed mine about a half hour ago. I'll never miss having an utterly tasteless piece of gum in my mouth to control my jaw. I'm not even chewing that gum, I'm grinding it to pieces. I will never miss the fear in my parent's faces when I was angry drunk. Absolutely volatile and frightening. It takes a lot to make me really angry...when I am....woohoo. I'll always hate the knuckle mark in my wall because I just felt like I needed to feel something, anything. Which is why I understand cutters, burners, etc. I'll never miss knowing just by the way I look, I did something awful. I'll never miss not knowing why my hand is bleeding. I'll never miss waking up in my boots under a stranger's coat. Face next to an over-packed ashtray and a table riddled with ashes and coke residue, looking across the room at a stranger curled up in a ball on a chair underneath my coat. That awful smell of stale smoke and cigarettes put out in a beer bottle or having the audacity to look at the empty baggies on the table to see if there's anything left. Knowing that if there was, I would actually start all over again, no matter how bad I felt. Knowing I left the house with $400.00 and re-entering the house with 8 pennies and an ATM receipt that reads UNAVAILABLE. I know for sure I've positively never assaulted anyone but myself. Ever the self-saboteur am I. I'm guessing you may have a hint of that lingering in your brain. I'll never miss losing one great friend after another...if I could, I'd just make one full chapter of names alone, followed by my sincerest apology, and I surely would. Well, it's my book...and I'll cry if I want to...cry if I....yep, just couldn't help myself ...maybe at the very end of this never ending story. I pray every day that the person I was is at peace. When that creepy tarot lady told me I had a demon inside of me...not too long after that was when I swallowed that bottle of blood pressure medication. Obviously, I would think by now, you know that my brain is a circus. It never stops. Even my dreams are so vivid, I have to really stop and think if it was real or not.

Weird things pop into my head, like making out in the woods with some boy in 8th grade and wondering why this just didn't seem quite right.

I wonder where words like pillow and blanket came from...and yet I will never research it because I like the mystery of it.

I think, for the very first time in my life, I love me. I love that I fought to save my life and realize I could start all over again. I learned I could be exactly who and what I want to be. Remember this, my dear friend, there is a strength in you that you just don't see.....yet. You are terrifically strong. Maybe you're having a bad day, a bad relationship, terrible pain that doesn't get the empathy you seek because you cannot imagine how crippling this pain can be, maybe you're unemployed. Maybe you've lost a spouse, a child, a sibling, mother, father far too soon. Maybe you've lost probably your best love...a pooch or a kitty. Maybe you just harbor hatred for someone and keep yourself locked in this cage...maybe you're just afraid....maybe you're sad...listen, LISTEN, tomorrow you might laugh. Tomorrow an old friend might reach out. We've all been in relationships that we were sure we'd never get over and never know how to live without this person...and guess what?! We surely did. A very brilliant teacher and mentor introduced me to, "give time, time." I've been where you are. It passes....brilliantly. You suddenly discover the part of your brain that learns to cope and deal with whatever ails you. When we isolate ourselves, we forget that there are people out there who would suffer greatly if they lost you. I don't mean just in death, I mean disappearing from the world. Canceling plans because of anxiety or loading up on Xanax to calm you down...only...it's calmed you down too much and you can't show up slurring. You'll have anxiety over being relaxed. If you feel so down for any reason and, you just can't shake it, understand you have a disease that can be treated. It's just like any other disease that you wouldn't ignore. If something causes you to hibernate all 4 seasons, you're sick. Get it out...cry, scream...tell someone what you feel and really hear their empathy because you are not alone. We are everywhere, darling. And I'll tell you what....

.....if this hot mess of a woman can not only be a certified alcohol and substance abuse counselor...but I'm alive. I tried to die and I failed because my plan is to hold you and love you until you can love yourself. My plan is to give the gifts that I've been given. The people who have taught me how to change my self destructive thinking and believe that I can and I will. I promise, with all of my heart, if you find a therapist, talk to your doctor, reach out to life and recovery coaches...even if it's just a friend you trust, get it out...your life will be anything you wish for. Your wildest dreams absolutely will come true. They did for me. Trust me.

**I've just stopped naming chapters....haven't I? Really I haven't been doing it all along...I'm just in denial**

Ah new love...sorry, sorry....ah, new like. At this age, who has time to waste? 15 minutes, you made me laugh, I looked at you for a second and felt like kissing you, let's plan our country wedding tomorrow...we're almost 40 for God's sake! I have a habit, admittedly, of dating straight women. Obviously, they're not totally straight, because I'm not that tempting and smooth to keep'em comin'. We've obviously been through my list of reasons why I just don't dig the whole lesbian scene. I'm not saying all lesbians are rotten, lying cheaters who wait for their best friends to go to the bathroom so they can make out with their best friends girlfriend. I'm also not saying I've never waited for someone's boyfriend or husband to hit the toilet before I asked her to come look underneath the bar for my contact lens or pacifier, whichever was more convenient at the time. Generally, most of the good ones, in any lifestyle, are taken....by their spouse and respective mistress or, uh...mastress?! Plate's full. You know when you're past the age of 32 and you want to stay on the phone with someone for longer than 20 minutes, this is your baby. This is the lid

for your pot, kid.


When you've met someone in your early 20's, they really

always look like they're in their early 20's because let's

face it, when we were in our early 20's in obscenely tight

clothes and obsessed over the fact that "I lookkkkk

ffaaaatttt.....do I look ffaaaattttt? Do these jeans make

me look fffaaatttt?! Does this tube top, mini skirt and

body glitter make me lookkkkk ffaaaattttt....ugh I'm so

fattttttt...." No, I never wore a tube top beyond the age

of 5 and even then, it was criminal. Besides my breasts

are way too big for tube top and at this age, you never

want to run the risk of looking like you're smuggling

coins in your boob bandage. We need support, girls.

Hold'em up, make'em look fantastic! When I saw women my age at a club when I was 21, I thought it was cute that the old ladies came out to dance. I never noticed they were long gone by 10 because by now I know they've been there since 8 and hour and a half is plenty. Too much in fact. I don't really remember if I thought they were kinda creepy or cute for being out. They always danced in that 2 step back and forth, snapping their fingers behind their back with their heads leaned back, dreamily looking at the ceiling. Now, in my head, I believe I'm a pretty good dancer....but I wonder if I'm doing that 2 step. They certainly didn't give a shit if they were the only ones on the dance floor. I'm definitely at that age where I also don't give a shit if no one is on the dance floor. When I was younger, chances are, I probably either pre-gamed it, was on some type of drug or behind a bar so I probably didn't give a shit about shaking my shimmy all by myself. There are those really delicious older women who are hungry for love who do a mom, hard seam of the jeans up their ass, too short and tapered at the ankle but not in a skinny jean type way. Rather. A douchebag with a belt. They'll be five of them that are wearing a turtleneck under their pretty sweater in a humping soul train knowing half the lyrics of Cher's "Dark Lady" and they'll reminisce about the gold old days....when they were soul train humming with the same 5 friends and aside from passing each other around after getting hammered, they wonder why they're still single and still say things like, "we'll find the one when we're not looking. She'll show up when we least expect it." Keep telling yourself that Brenda. But while you're still dry humping Kate, Jan, Roberta (who everyone calls Bert) and Cappy, Mrs. Right is walking

passed you to use the bathroom. Maybe once a year, I'll

go to some sort of "ladies" party and I'll still see those

women and in the rare instance they unhook and they

know someone I might be chatting with and I'm

introduced to them I feel compelled to say, "yeah, I've

seen you in every picture, in every gallery, on every

website, for every lesbian function....since 1986. You're

famous!!!" Even as I get older and admire the age and

the desire to maybe hit the dance floor once in a blue

moon, I will still pity the fab 5. Their families have had

interventions more than 20 times in the last 24 years.

They eternally enable one another and say things like,

"real family are the ones you choose." And they'll curse

about their family to Cappy because she listens the best

while polishing off a bottle of jack and waking up with

two cats on your chest. One has some sort of mange and the other mysteriously walks on only 2 legs...dragging the rest behind him. The hard jeans outlining their entire anatomy under a crocheted blanket that has never been washed while Cappy shuffles around in her oversized slippers making coffee with a cigarette dangling from her lips. Blanket jeans will wake up with a raspy voice and say something stupid like, "I feel like I might be getting the flu. My throat is sore and my head is killing me. I'm all sweaty and my hands are clammy." It has nothing at all to do, Brenda, with the 8 pint glasses of jjjaaaaaaaaaaack...and a splash of coke and the pack and a half of cigarettes you smoked while slurring to Cappy that you love her because she understands you..."sshhheeee allwwwaaaayyyzzzzzzzdid! Howwww come...how come...howwwww commmeee, Cap, you and me, me and you never got married?! We, we

we...you know mmeeee better than aannnnyyoonneeee

ellsseeee, Cap...Cappy. Howww come?!" Now, Cappy

will sit their silently with a cocky smirk on her face

because she knows she's a stud in her oversized slippers

and elastic ankle sweatpants and 34 year old hoodie that

says P-town athletic department that she wears

every...single....day. She also wears running shoes with

every outfit and is the type that will also rock the hard

tuck of her crisp, big collared, man's dress shirt into her

jeans, with dirty running sneakers to a formal function

and find that because she's got that snappy shirt on,

she's dressed up. She also believes that everyone knows

she's cool enough to wear jeans to her nieces wedding.

And yet still, some elderly aunt will ask her when she's

gonna meet a nice fella and settle (pronounced seh-il)

down.

**Little tangent.**

Personally, I find that older women look and are sexier. However, few feel that way. One comment that is constantly thrown my way is, "man, you used to be so...mmmmmm..." Man, I used to be so"mmmmm?!" And now what? I'm "blech!"?! I get that more often than not and I don't think people realize how hurtful it is. My self esteem at this age is certainly much more intact than it was then...because I always thought I looked fffaaaaaaaaatttt (this is all in a whiny voice, in case you're not reading it properly.) As an adult, I'm overweight. Not grossly overweight but overweight nonetheless. I have some type of old lady odd hair growth that I'm not ashamed to admit because I spend 18 hours every 2 days tweezing it and for anything to take me that much work...you're going to hear about it....and you're going to like it. Men, I dare you to pluck every hair out by a tweezer one at a time. See how tough a woman really is.

If by happenstance something "happens" between us,

which is not likely, because I don't even care about sex

anymore, and I have to sleep over, I will act mysteriously

and leave just before the sun comes up. I'll make you

believe I either have the only Sunday doctor's

appointment on the continent or that I'm still that much

of a stud and slipping it out is just another way for you

to feel "hungry" for me. Fact is, I'll have at least one

unusual chin hair that will either have to come out or I

will be incessantly touching it. And ladies, if you don't

know other ladies realize that you're not only constantly

touching it but rather trying to violently pinch it out of

your face, you're mistaken. Most of us are just classy

enough to not call another woman out on her one

wicked witch hair. If I stay later than the sun coming up,

I will talk to you with my chin almost on my chest and

you will think I'm a weird character anyway. Now, this is

a one at a time process. Clearly it's not even remotely as

much as a man's beard but, try to imagine a man not

shaving in the morning rather pulling each individual

hair out with a tweezer. That's dedication to the cause

right there. I'm a little psychotic about it so my neck is

slightly scarred and now everyone who comes within 10

feet of me will test the theory. I realize that I see it as far

worse than it is. But, you seem I don't cheat. take...if

you'd like for any person who's kissing you to have rug

burn after and be completely turned off to have a

second kiss. If I wanted to feel the roughness of a

dude...well, guess what? Yep...I'd be with a dude. I

know, beyond a shadow of a doubt, that many of my

friends enjoy the roughness of a 5 o'clock shadow. On a

woman, however...not so much. You might want to consider waxing, laser, threading, pulling, duct tape, crazy glue and a leather strap...anything else at all other than shaving. The secrecy of my life....it just doesn't exist anymore. A lady will never tell you she has facial hair....I just told you about my facial hair. Ladies...should you plan on kissing another lady....don't shave.


**Rush hour foot traffic**

Please put down the nook, the book, the cell phone, the iPad, the iPod, the newspaper, your mother...please recognize that the sidewalk is 59ft wide so, there is virtually no reason you should cause me to slam into a wall...which, by the way, I do like a champ. When you're with a group (which I think, personally, it should be against the law for tourists to be out on the street between 7am - 9am and 4:00pm -6pm) and you're all walking like a 7 person wall with a few rebellious stragglers in the back, it makes it wildly impossible to get around you which means...I walk in the street in downtown Manhattan WAY too much. If you happen to be taking a photograph, don't leave a 96ft gap between you and your model only to find as I walk by, that the picture you took...was a close up of her face. The photo team act as kind of a dam that's backing up quickly and ready to explode (and people say New Yorkers are rude. If we're willing to hold up a line of 10,594 people so that you can take a picture of your wife in front of the Bull statue by the ferry, then we are the kindest, most patient people on earth...until you have that one guy who's run/walking, all but yelling into his Bluetooth who shoots right out in front of this botched attempt at making memories. Once that guy crosses over the threshold, just about everyone takes it as a green light and off we go. I'm usually the ninny who still continues to wait until this masterpiece is complete. There should be a law that if you can't walk 36mph, then you are positively only allowed to stay inside of the Empire State Building slow walking up and down the stairs. For your own safety, if you don't know how to bob and weave out of rush hour walking traffic, you're bound for a game of "RED ROVER...RED ROVER....WE CALL TOURIST RIGHT OVER..." that you weren't anticipating.

Yes, I do believe they should wait until after we heavy bag carrying, over tired, overworked New Yorkers find their way to their clock to punch.  Or maybe, Mayor

Bloomberg (sipping my Big Gulp) you should screw the

bike lane since no cyclist uses it. They'd much rather

make you think you're coming within an inch of your life

before turning the wheel just in time to make you think

that your spine has locked and clearly this is your

demise. You attempt to yell "YOU SON OF A BITCH?!"

But Humpty Dumpty is already half a mile away

terrorizing other pedestrians with his chicken style

cycling. Anyhoo, Mayor Bloomy (another sip of my Big

Gulp) go ahead and make that the tourist lane. This way

the tourist won't interfere with people who are walking

down the block 100 miles per hour. Swerving in and out

of pedestrian traffic like a NASCAR Driver. Rush hour is

not for the sensitive, bike fearing citizens. Nobody wants

to feel the wrath of BIKEMAN.

What I don't get is, why Wall Street? I mean, I get that Wall Street is a household name however, if I was a tourist did enough homework to find out how to get to Beaver Street, I would also know that the people who work on Beaver Street are probably not the friendliest group of people on earth. Especially during rush hour. For a living (trading room) people are a bit aggressive. When you're zig zagging in front of them to take a picture next to the doorman as if he is not a living being. I promise you, he wants to wrap you in the back of your head and the traders basically want to kill you. Now, for the rest of us who know to really kinda switch lanes like a pro, we know the strung out eyes of a trader and to get as far left as humanly possible. We also would like to clothesline you while you're zig zagging in front of us and we have 3 minutes to get to the train that we will inevitably missed because you had to get a picture of your girlfriend of three months in front of some scaffolding (and she will pose like this is going in a magazine. She'll make it her Facebook profile picture for well over a year and her friends from Iceland will be so jealous that they didn't get to strike a pose in front of that fabulous scaffolding). Don't get me wrong, we love the 2 billion tourists that come a month because it keeps our economy up and makes it entirely possible for us to all be 10 minutes late to work even if we've left at 4am to make it to a 10am job.....that is really 45 minutes from door to door. Perhaps our local government can set up tourist skyways so that can marvel in the wonder that is the rush hour animal. You can hear the oohs and aahs as they point wide eyed and say, "Look at that one, dad! It's 12 degrees out and that man is just wearing a shirt with the sleeves rolled up and a tie loosened at the neck and it says here on the info board that he chain smokes half a pack of cigarettes by 8:42 am....ooh ooh and look, there's the messy haired lesbian - she's of the lip ringed breed and it says here that she could eat up to 52 oxycodone plants a day - this one here went to rescue farm and was released back into the wild after a tough battle with literally throwing a chain around her neck and having 12 strong zookeepers yank her away from the oxycodone tree. They say this very rare breed VERY RARE mates for life and aawwwww...she lost her companion a little while ago. Science has tried to intervene and slowly introduce this Lesbosaurus Rex to a different companion, this far she has eaten ones head, ripped another ones heart clear out of its chest and carried the third off to the breed that has absolutely no ability to remain monogamous and dropped her there to

isle of seedy corner bar. MOM MOM look...there's the

exhibit you've been looking for!!! It's the barracuda

business woman who wears $12,000 suits to bed. They

say this one here has a Bluetooth for an ear and talks

obsessively loud and says the word, "FUCK" a lot.

Parental discretion is advised. Here we have the sweater

vested underpaid cold caller. This population flourishes

in all communities because it's fed a steady diet of

cocaine and Red Bull. This sign reads, "Please do not

feed the angry feminist vegan. She will not only tear

your limbs off but she will scream at you for things like

Vietnam and the Manson family no matter how young

you are. She will blame you and call you things like

fascist and commie and she will have no idea what

either mean. She'd have just heard it in some movie

starring Jane Fonda in short shorts and thought it sounded tough and intelligent. Besides there is nothing you have on you that she will be able to eat. It must be soy, dairy, gluten, air and water free and what do you know…you just polished off your last sip of hot air and you're far too afraid to get close enough to tell her. Her and the bike messenger are getting married next month. Planning on having a bunch of angry, starving, extreme sports babies so they can take over the city….and they'd be successful because we know deep in our hearts, we'd have a better chance of getting a sparerib bone out of the mouth of a grizzly in your backyard. If you don't have a backyard and you're a city person, think of holding a handful of something like sunflower seeds next to a homemade pigeon coop that's door is just about ready to fly open. That's what Mr. and Mrs. Veganger are like on a friendly day. Honeymoon starts on the war bike

flying through the streets. Keep a close eye out.

**...if that new person you're dating seems a little funny**

**(in a not so funny way) guess what? Yep. They'll stay**

**nice and funny too..matter of fact, they'll get**

**downright hilarious...**

I have an unusual spinal injury brought on by a punch

from a psychopath ex (I don't even like to acknowledge

she was an ex because she's a disgusting abusive

animal...yeah, a lot of us have been there. Special note:

if your spouse is the kind of jerk off who likes to punch

holes in walls, doors, Chinese room separators of which I

don't know the name of at this very moment...chances

are they're going to graduate to true asshole status and,

you will have bruises one day. I recommend you pack up

your special stuff and say, "see ya 'round, Kong!")

Anyway, not the point...fact is, because I'm a Recovery

Coach and an Alcohol and Substance Abuse Counselor, I

have to refuse pain medications or any narcotic because

they really are high on the list of my drug of choice and

it's just not worth the trial anymore. I tried it last year

and I found that I wasn't necessarily following the "every

8 hours" maybe occasionally the every 2 hour rule (who

am I kidding?) sounded much more enjoyable.

Henceforth...it is in my best interest to grit my teeth and

say, "no thank you, I'll take Ibuprofen." I may as well be

eating a box of tic tacs and calling it a day. But, I'm

dedicated to what I do and I would never help someone

climb out of the awful hole they're in while being a

hypocrite. Not a chance. So, I've been going to the same pain management clinic to get an epidural which is so delicious and pleasant, especially when you hear the crunch of your spine getting pierced by this absurd needle. In any event, it takes the pain away completely and the attending nurse, in order to keep me calm, I believe thinks she rubbing my legs but is always rubbing my ass. It feels delightful, I admit....so, I'll take the Bic pen sized needle into my vertebrae. I've been going for 2 years and for whatever reason, I still need to get a consultation which goes a little like this: "Hey, Sar!" "Hey there! How's your daughter? The cat's hair ball issue? Did you get the new food I told you about?" "I did! It's awesome! Thank you! So, don't take any ibuprofen or eat 6 hours before the shot!" "Yep, got it." "Ok...we'll see you in a month."

I'm going to go to Congress to make sure that they change the label on muscle relaxers (not a narcotic, by the way) to say, "Will make you involuntarily walk like you're doing the electric slide without warning." Brushing my teeth is a chore and when I try to put my bra on, I start gasping for air. Yes, I realize I have a set that requires work to strap in but not enough to leave me winded. I'll sit down and look around until I realize I have to put a shirt on...so I'll basically do something that looks like my floor has rearranged itself into a small hill...and run down it, sideways. I have 3 open doors in my room and one treacherous set of stairs that everyone has fallen down at one point. And this isn't the heel slip I discussed in the beginning of the book...If you lose your footing on these babies...better remember the Hail Mary cause you're going down. The outside of these magnificent steps are surrounded by basically 6 planks which would act only as a reminder that there are stairs there. You crash into this shoddy attempt at protection, you're crashing through and falling to your death or a severely broken leg. Needless to say, I've learned on muscle relaxers to dry to avoid the stairway area which is tough if you want to eat or do peepees or get up and go to your very important job. What I do not do, however, is avoid those three open gateways to hell. I made it by one open orifice in an attempt to continue to pile more stuff on top of any already 8 foot mountain of underwear. (I just keep buying more of the fancy packaged ones...I know only one person touched them.) Because I am incapable of transporting this pile down these vertical steps...and if you want to discuss deadly, go take a trip down my winding basement steps without a railing into the Blair Witch basement. Anyone with an old house knows about these fascinating little extras. Pedestal sinks with one faucet for hot and one for cold. It takes the hot about 4 minutes to get hot but when it gets hot it gets HOT so you have to rapidly keep jetting your hands back and forth so as to avoid scolding or hypothermia. Claw tub that you really should have at least a step ladder to get in and out of because not only is it 5 feet deep, it's 3 feet off the floor. I have a toilet that flushes twice, which I suppose is clever....although I'm not quite sure why it does that. I guess we like to keep everything unique. Old houses also come with a very fancy extra of a bolt of lightning shooting out of the light switch when you try to turn it on. By now, everyone is so used to being flat out electrocuted, we've just all

found our method of keeping the searing pain to a bare

minimum if possible. If your house is really old, you'll

have that little push button switch that I firmly believe

came with the electric shock as part of the package.

Most of the light fixtures in the house have to be turned

on by one of those hanging metal chains and they

generally feel like they're just gonna plum fall right out

of the ceiling onto your head. And please tell me what

household doesn't come standard with a light switch

that leads to positively nothing. Flick it on and off all day,

buddy...you will never get a reason for the phantom

light switch. My parents best housekeeping tip is don't

move or touch anything at all, and then we won't need

to clean it. Just a quick sssswwiisshhh of a duster and

we're all set. I've also discovered that there is no real

reason for every single door in the house sound like a Vincent Price movie. If you're regularly skittish, you'd never last one night. I've woken up to people who have looked so overtired and strung out, I was most convinced they left the bed in the middle of the night to go hit a crack pipe and slid menacingly back. And no, I don't mean someone I "brought home", I mean a friend because, again, there is nothing sexier than inviting a girl back to your parents house. We do have those fancy, unpainted oak doors with, what looks like Swarovski crystal but it feels more like clear plastic. These all come with one skeleton key. We officially have only one left and my mother is so crazy about those doors and fixtures in order to maintain the classic antiquity of the house. This means should one of us had lost the key somehow after locking the door on your side and you're that screwed in the head that you can't find it (even after you're the only one n the locked side of the door) mother would basically, "oh well.....you break it you bought it!" While sliding one potato chip at a time and shooting a water pistol through the open lock that should have a key in it, for you water supply. I'm sure if I asked, she'd sing. Going back to being electrocuted. When I was little and I mean 3, 4, 5, my little family consisting of my mother who closely resemble Morla from The Neverending Story in her actions and speech (if some of you have no clue who I'm talking about, I recommend maybe YouTube-ing Morla - now my mother is 4'6, 67 lbs soaking wet (obviously I'm exaggerating. She's at least 72 lbs and is convinced, as I had said that her clothes are growing. You do have to wait about 15 seconds after you've asked something for her to either turn to you and say,

"aalllrrriiggghhhtttt...take a bbreeeattthhhh....what's the

mmaaattteeerrrr?" Meanwhile, back at the ranch, she

only thinks you're upset because you're talking at a

normal speed and to her, that's too exciting. You have to

verbally say, after 15 seconds, "Are you going to answer

me? *no response* MOM, ANSWER ME!" She's an

exceptionally smart woman and retired from Verizon

after helping people out with their electronics for 25

years (really moving with the times and watching it

evolve). Try to get her to set an alarm clock for 9:30am

when it's only going to scare the shit out of you because

it just randomly goes off at 9:30pm. You're not sure

what you're hearing but you know you hear mumbling

and, in that convincingly haunted house, you freeze and

lock your body into an "I'm going to pee my pants I'm so

scared!" Mode. If she had to put the time on a DVD player, it would eternally blink 12:01 am. Thank God for cell phones and cable boxes otherwise no one in that house would know truly what time it is. You know what else is a humdinger of a good time? And I will absolutely guess a lot of you will share in this party with me. Being in the passenger seat of a car that your mother is driving. *sigh*. Being IN the car that your MOTHER is responsible for operating. You first must locate all of the "OH SHIT" handles. These are the handles in the ceiling which seem to serve only 2 purposes. 1. To hang dry cleaning on and B. For a passenger in the car to grab onto every time she's with a particularly peculiar driver (my mother gets highly offended when I say she's a terrible driver so, just between you and I, my mother can't drive to save her life...sshhh). Always fun to be in car with a person who perpetually goes no more than 17 mph. She's little so, all you really ever see is the very tip of her head and white gripped knuckles on 10 and 2 with the seat just about an eighth of an inch from the steering wheel. Which works beautifully when you quickly go out to move her car and don't realize it until it's too late. I once spent an entire weekend trapped between the windshield and the dashboard. I tried beeping the horn but my only good arm fell through a grate and landed in the glove compartment. They only found me because I was wearing a scarf they couldn't find. A windfall of road rage follows her. My mother has been called some of the most colorful names in the world. Some of them I think are made up they're so angry. Now, try to go around her. She's that annoying woman you're walking behind when you're in a rush.

Christmas Eve last minute shopping *shaking my head...tears streaming down my face.) She will slowly strut up to the register. 987 waiting in line. Now it's her turn. She'll go through every item individually and tell the cashier the story about where she found it and what the sign said. Then one of the articles of clothing will have a brown mark or something. She'll begin to rub the stain with her thumb and stare at it while the cashier and I grill her. Both of us are dying to yell, "FUCKING SERIOUSLY??!!!!" But if we do that, she'll get offended and that will tack on another 12 minutes. The girl very politely asks, "Do you want that shirt!" Now, we've all learned that on most occasions, it is necessary to tell her that she has to answer you. Of course, this cashier doesn't know that so she's basically staring at my mother. Growing more heated with each passing second. Let us not forget that an angry mob is forming behind us. They're wrapping t-shirts around wooden hangers and squeezing out the sponge of lighter fluid from the guy who's third to last's Zippo. My mother remains. Undaunted. Then to make it worse, she'll turn around and do that sinister laugh thinking everyone will laugh along with her. This is where I jump in because I want my mother around for Christmas. I basically box her out and start answering for her. She will attempt to go into her purse to get her wallet which will also take another 8 minutes. Like a ninja, I snatch the wallet out, which makes her mad because she has yet to realize that I'm saving her life. I give the cashier that, "WE GOT THIS!" look and turn into action figures. "No ma'am it's 2013. I didn't even know people had personal checks anymore. Fascinating! Can I see one?!" She also, clever little shrew, would also take that golden opportunity to balance her checkbook and then read the receipt that's 14 miles long, convinced that she'll find something. Ok, so cashier packs the bag, I swipe the card, put in the pin, and hear her take that breath you take before you start to speak...immediately interject with, "gift boxes please!" This dumb broad was obviously not paying attention when she said, "how many and what sizes?" You asshole. See! I was trying to do something nice and for all of us. Throw a damn corrugated box full of all shapes and sizes and hope for the best. I basically gave her a look, "oh well, bud. You're on your own." My mother's is the only car I'll ever ride in that has an imaginary accelerator that I start slamming on. She can't drive on the highway because God forbid a detour took her into any other lane but the right, we'd be in North

Dakota before she was able to stop and that's only because there's some barren stretch of road there that has a sign that reads "THE END". I managed to convince her that the sign is literal and tell her what a fabulous time she did and how much rest she should get for getting us well passed our destination safely. Just as a favor to her, of course, why don't you let me have a whack at driving us home and you just rest your pretty little head *pat pat pat on the head* Once she begins to argue with me, it is at that point where I turn to my dear loving mother, my best friend in life, the woman I owe my life to and tell her, "give me the fucking keys right now or I leave your skinny ass out here in the middle of nowhere. She'll suck her teeth at me and hand them right over. Not because she knows I would leave her anyway it's because by my responding somewhat hastily means she won this race. My parents are so damn competitive. It's exhausting. Keeps me on my "choose your battles" toes. As you get older, you truly realize the importance of that phrase. Silence speaks a whole lot louder than words, my friend.

So...the point of Christmas, electrocuted, my mother....when I was about 4 or 5, as is the case with any kid at or around that age, Christmas is MAGIC! You mean all I have to do is wait for someone else's birthday and I'll get a mountain of gifts under a sparkly tree? Fantastic! Well, I always wanted the tree on and really wanted to be the only person to turn it on. You see, old house living during the wrap up of my parents hippy stage, living in a pretty big fixer upper, trivial things like the 4 year old climbing under the tree. Plugging in the tree, night after night with high hopes and watching 4 of

July explode out the socket and have me jump up and yell, "SOMETHING BIT ME!!!" Night after night, I thought we had a squirrel in the tree that would fight me because we stole his home. I tried to reason with him that we made his home pretty and that we look at it every day and it makes us smile and you get all the free candy canes you want. Well, that damn squirrel still bit me night after night. I also couldn't understand why the bite would make it feel like I was flexing my muscles like MACH MACHO MMAAANNNN. Chalking it up to my parent's youth, I realize now that none of us didn't realize that some sockets just do that. So, if the treat works and lights up, we guess it's not broken. And the feeling of being bitten they just thought it was because I was sliding my arm into the faux pine needles to get to the plug. Nothing like those gigantic, Peanuts like lights on the tree. The whole big bulb that could be unscrewed when needed to be replaced. (I think we went a little bit backwards as far as now having one little shitty bulb that knocks out the string. And I dare anyone, except for the creators, to tell me that they have successfully replaced one of those bulbs without breaking the glass piece and leaving the plastic stuck in the hole and having it actually make the rest of the bulbs turn back on.) It's a conspiracy. So, here I am just barely out of toddler world, having regular shock treatments and making sure that when I unplugged it that night, that those oversized peanuts lights made it comfortably across my arms when they were at their peak 538 degree 4th degree burn worthy state. A 6, I looked like a cutter, a burner and someone with the "mom cut my bangs incredibly crooked the night before my school picture day...so the only option is to try as much as possible to make it part to the side which in turn turns out to be a curling iron burned bang. The only other option was to cut my bangs completely off and let my long blonde hair cascade my back while the front looked like there was either a helicopter sized fan was constantly blowing my hair back or quite possibly, to go along with my Christmas light scars, the bangs have been singed off as well. In any event, I still have my 3rd, 4th and 5th grade 8 x 10's where I'm rocking my cockeyed bangs. See how this played out in my adulthood? I've continued to make my hair look as cockeyed as possible. I thought moms were the only people in the world who cut our hair. And it only took my speedy mother 4 hours to cut my bangs so beautifully. Dear woman, if you're every behind my mother walking, I will give you this snippet of advice:

either crawl over counters and people to get in front of

her or be prepared to feel the kind of shaking rage that

makes you feel like you want to scream loud enough for

her to answer without having to ask her to answer - she

won't answer you anyway. Just know that if you're

behind her, she goes so slow, you feel like you're

walking backwards. I've tried for many years to get her

to be able to cross one whole street before the "walk"

sign turned to "don't walk no more than 2 times. Sadly,

my mother has to stand straight up like a stick so as to

allow the 5th line of cars whiz by her. I stand on the curb

looking through my fingers covering my eyes. By the

time we do meet up, I look like I'm ready to collapse

from exhaustion and she looks perfectly relaxed. I long

to be 1/16 as calm as she is. For every mind numbingly

walk or drive I've ever taken with my mother, I'd have to

say, she certainly flew into action when I needed her.

Today, my mother and I laugh about how painstaking it is to get her to pick out a birthday card...and I think one of the only reasons we can do that is because I'm still here to buy her one and I'm still here for her to spend 9hours and 4 announcements of "please bring your final purchases to the front" later. Next year, though, she's plugging those damn lights in.

## This really doesn't belong anywhere

Some days seem like they just can't possibly get any worse. Some days go on and on with no end in sight. Ever look at someone on the train, bus, ferry, rickshaw, bowling alley and you can just tell they've been crying.

You can tell by the furious way they pinch the top of their nose between their eyes that they're either doing anything to stop crying or they have a horrendous migraine or in cases like mine, they refuse to sneeze in public and will all but slap themselves in the face in order to prevent such a catastrophe. I know, personally, that if I'm in the verge of tears and someone either asks me what's wrong, are you ok?, do you know what time it is?, do you have 4 quarters? Basically anything is going to bring my waterworks to the forefront and with a vengeance. What would happen, though....what would it kill us if maybe someday we see this sad little sack of potatoes in front of us and we maybe just reached out our hand and patted them on the back or the arm and just gave them that kind of reassuring nod that meant, "It'll all be ok, soon." Unless that person is dangerously antisocial, the danger in empathy doesn't run too deep. Please don't get me wrong...if this person you seek to just acknowledge decides to hot crack you in the mouth, I don't want to take full responsibility for your assault. Be mindful of who you're about to console. If this person is yelling, "I shot Abraham Lincoln!!! I DID IT AND I KNOW IT!!" Hold off on the, "I've been there, fella." Back pat. Frankly because, well, you haven't been there and secondly because well, you haven't been there. There are some moments where I feel like maybe telling the soulful crier, "gee, I don't know what you're listening to in those headphones of yours but, my guess is it's a step up from monks chanting, "Jump off the ledge....jjuuummpppp off the lleeeddggggeeee." Why don't we just go ahead and pocket the iPod and discover the sounds of nature. In our nature sounds are...horns blaring, the rat a tat tat of an oversized drill, Turkish

delight at the falafel stand, the sweet sound of a mother

with her child in the armpit death grip growling, "if you

run out in front of me again...I'm going to throw you

down a manhole." Sweet things...things that make your

day flowery. Anything but the wedding song for the

wedding you're not going to have (with this particular

person. You'll have a wedding and a song...just a

different party waiting down the end for you)

**You say it your birthday (bew nu nu nu bew uh) *that's my version of an air guitar* it's my birthday too!!!**


Today...I am 38 years old. I kind of go back and forth on the notion of how I feel about aging. And no, I don't mean I see myself as an octogenarian, I mean literally getting older. I was driving yesterday to see my nieces traveling basketball game. The trip in and of itself was close to 2 hours long but, to walk into that crowded gym with many faces and see her spot me right away and so excitedly smile makes me realize that while I was thinking how absurd it was to drive 2 hours away to see 9 and 10 year olds play basketball, it was probably one of the least absurd things I've done all year. There is nothing in the world, as far as I'm concerned, to see a child light up with so much joy just to see your face. Now, this isn't dopey basketball at all. These girls play like they're in high school so it gets pretty intense. All 3 of my kids play sports with the kind of tenacity their father did (brother played professional baseball) so it's really important for them to pay attention. Well, when I have to tell that wonderful little girl to turn around to face the game because she's that excited to see me,

then I truly know what a lucky woman I am. So anyway,

I'm driving. The route I'm taking is a route I used to take

all the time to go to a ladies party. Which means, yes, it

is a lesbian tea party. I'm looking around as I'm driving at

all of these landmarks that are so familiar and I

remember being in a car full of girls or possibly just my

girlfriend at the time in our way to a perfect, cater to all

bar. One room a dance floor, one a regular bar with a

jukebox, an outside deck and it was a damn good time.

Now, the song "Send Me on My Way" by Rusted Root

comes on and it actually made my throat feel like it was

closing because this was a song that became the

"everyone is feeling a good buzz" anthem. The wave of

nostalgia that fell over me was so difficult to

differentiate between whether it was a good feeling or a

bad feeling. So now, all of my senses less taste are on fire. My strongest sense is my sense of smell, always. Which is very tough because you can't turn that off. Every other sense you can basically avoid. Unless you cut your nose off to spite your face, you're screwed with smell. I could smell that familiar scent of winter becoming spring. I can almost smell the sunset. I smell tires on a road close to country land. Yes, it's that intense. One after another are songs that are either a good or bad memory. However, even when it's a good memory, it's a memory nonetheless and generally that could make anyone melancholy. At that moment, I feel my age and the time that has passed me by but, I also realize that I'm not only very young but have been given the great opportunity to start over. I know there was at least a block of really excellent times with really fantastic people. The decline came so quickly. Nothing was fun anymore. Even when I thought I was having fun, I was a hot drunk mess waiting on line for the bathroom to shovel coke up my nose. I guess I'd have to say, I wouldn't go back to my late 20's early 30's at all. And when I think of 20 something, I think of how utterly stupid yet wonderfully carefree I was. All this being said while sniffing the air like a dog waiting for all 26 lbs of Thanksgiving turkey to hit the floor, I just about miss my turn. What do I do? Just go a little bit down the road and make a u-turn or, do I cut across 10 lanes of whipping traffic to hang a hard enough right that I was sure I'd have a rollover...and do I do this in front of a high school? Operative word SCHOOL.

Well, I gathered myself up after my NASCAR worthy turn and realized that's the ticket. Therein lies the answer. Thinking too much about your past can be very dangerous. It can prevent you from making the right choices and assure you that you will miss good times and the way a 9 year old lights up to just see you there to cheer her on. I'll leave the country asphalt and Rusted Root to a new generation of 20 something's to have the same kind of fun I did. My good times consist of safety, of the present, my friends and most importantly, my family. Had a burned rubber on that asphalt, it could have been the end. A lot of those hard turns could have been the last.

So, I'm gonna slow down and find an alternate route. I'll make sure I have the right detour signs blinking bright neon telling me that I need to, next time, take a smooth left and just find a new way to my destination. A word of advice: there are other people around you on this road. They're staying pretty close because they're following your lead. If you don't ease onto the brakes and use your blinker to alert them that you're going to speed and be reckless, you're liable for taking the whole crew down with you. Use the parts that God has given you so you and your support don't become a precession. Copy?

Anyhow, the whole point of this book, even though I realize it can get very dark at some points, it's to remind you of why we should take things nice and slow. 38

years ago a small person appeared into bright lights in a freezing cold room. She had spiky hair and a questionable attitude. That baby looked around that room and became frustrated that she couldn't relay her true feelings of uncomfortableness because, well, she couldn't speak yet. Bit of a language barrier. She wondered who would put such a heavy head onto such a tiny neck and shoulders. Basically a bobble head. 37 years, this little person made it a strict point to wreak havoc on the world and cause everyone to worry well beyond a reasonable amount. For 37 years, this person was just about destined for an early demise. Well, today that title girl knows how to speak and she probably does way too much of it. She still has spiky hair and a questionable attitude, and every time that this little girl enters into an overly bright, ultimately freezing room, she'll seek out a doctor to scream at. Most importantly ...this little girl now knows how to hold her own head up high because she finally has a backbone.

I think it's something that's heavily scripted for allow us to assume that getting another year older is a scary, bad day. Yes factually it is another day closer to death but how morbid is that? I would go back to my twenties to save my life. Maybe I'd spend one teenage day with my group of teenage friends because they were an excellent group of people. I like creeping up on 40. However, had I not changed my life this way, if I hadn't gotten sober and found a career, chances are, no, I wouldn't be happy about that. I would be a nervous wreck and convince myself that it's too late. It's a distinct possibility that I just wouldn't have made it. Harm at my own hands because, again, you somehow convince yourself that everyone would be better off if you were no longer alive.

I started writing this when I was 35. I'd really love to know how the hell James Patterson busts 800 books out a month. I was going to say Stephen King but once he made the scariest clown in history turn into a robot spider, invented some alien kid with a speech impediment have a group of geeks call him Dudditz because he couldn't say Douglas and had a character killed off because he needed to lean forward on a toilet bowl to grab a toothpick....I just figured he wasn't really writing anymore just kind of wandering around with a headset on babbling whatever bullshit popped into his head. How do you write classics like Carrie, The Shining, Stand By Me....so many classics, and then write 18 back to backs about the little guy always getting bullied by the 1950's greaser ....wait a minute...ok, well, there wasn't a 50's greaser in The Shining that I'm aware of.

Anyway, as I was saying. It's taken me 3 years to tell you my story. Let's keep in mind, I was smart enough to not try to write while I was drunk because I knew I made positively no sense. That was really my entire 35th year. I like to remind myself of why I never touched this book while I was drinking by going back to my Facebook posts just around that time. I'm posting things in Italian which means I consciously went out of my way to translate something to Italian because that's a clever way of exposing my assholeishness without anyone else being able to understand it. Only half of my friends are Italian and could at least figure out a word or two, most of my friends speak Spanish and they're relatively close and all of my friends know that you can translate anything in the world by copying and pasting on any one of the 4 billion free translation sites. Meanwhile...if I meant to say, "This is the hour of my demise!" (drama queen, I know) and did not realize that these sites translate things into a proper language, I was probably posting something like, "Today I will eat a rotten piece of cauliflower and it shall make me fall asleep with bleeding cuticles and a burnt out light bulb!" And that just isn't the mark I was looking to hit. I'm surprised I wasn't posting videos of myself on YouTube drunk singing, "Is This Love" by Whitesnake through my overly red, puffed up, stained red wine mouth.

The fact is I'm not entirely sure I was ever really clinically depressed, anxious or agoraphobic - because within about a week and a half of not drinking at all, all of those things seemed to lift. Hence, Alcohol Induced Psychosis. Clearly I was sad. Clearly I was angry but, clearly I had a lot going on in my head, my life and the banged up world I was creating for myself. You see, the point of this book is to tell you that suicide is NEVER the answer. Tomorrow IS another day and it positively does get better if you fight for it. Once you let the fight in you die, you die. I know it goes deeper than that but, that's the gist of it. When I tell you that I know and can very plainly see that I have done a 180, I did it with style. This was

not just 3 years of my life in the toilet. This was more

like 20 years. I'm 38 years old and I'm just now starting

my life. Things do change. When I tell you I was

teetering in the brink of death and I don't mean that

lightly, I mean one foot and one arm and half of my head

in the grave. The other half of my head, other arm and

leg finally woke up from a nap and discovered its

counterpart hanging in the dirt and finally said, "WHOA

THERE KID!!! GET UP!" No, the world is not better with

you gone, yes people will be devastated over it...they'll

also be angry with you. Maybe they'll be sad in the

beginning but I promise you this, when all the hubbub

dies down, they will be angry with you. Angry with you

for not reaching out, for not listening to them when they

told you they love you repeatedly, for still reaching out

to you when you were a sad sack and not much else, for even entertaining those texts and phone calls and yet STILL you gave up?! I wasn't angry with myself when I tried to kill myself 3 years ago, I was embarrassed and sorry. Now, I'm certified in preventing this in other people. Now, I am standing in front of you and I'm screaming, "WHOA THERE KID!!! GET UP!" Because today is not your day. You'll be dead one day, I promise. How about just letting nature run its course and you find out what plan was laid out for you. I'm sitting in an office getting paid to motivate people and I'm writing a book. Seriously?! 38 years old and my life is just starting now. At the very last crucial second, I opened my eyes a little wider and found out what the plan was for me. It's to save you. It's to tell you it's not a pretty white light when you close your eyes this way, it's dark and it's done. It's sadder than the living sad and the despair doesn't leave you. I hated every single ounce of me...except for that one little fighter cell in my body who took over just in the nick of time. Can you honestly sit there and tell me not one thing in life makes you happy? Not one? I won't lie to you, it's not an easy road. It's hard work, man. You don't just *POOF* turn around and become giddy with joy. But one day you do wake up and think, "ooh....holy shit...I feel ok." It's subtle and it's wonderful.

I want you here. I don't think for one second that the shoes you're walking in are not uncomfortable. I don't believe that things in your life haven't lead you to this kind of sadness. I want you here. I want you alive to laugh with me, to cry with me, to find the anger in you to drive you back to life. To watch that anger lift. One of the first things my therapist told me is, "we need to get to source of all of this rage." You would have thought I walked into a room growling and hissing at people when really I was doing quite the opposite. I was the clown everywhere I went. I was silly and ridiculous but, a brilliant person who paid attention saw how I really felt in my eyes. Every day I had a new reason for the source of the rage. I was bullied in school. When I came out, I wasn't accepted. I love someone who doesn't love me. People are gossiping terribly about me. I'm being held responsible for an entire group splitting up. My family hates me. I'm a drunk and a drug addict. I'm too overweight and it's gotten so far, I know I'll always be overweight now. I hate sunny days because they make me feel guilty for not getting out of bed. I can't get out of bed. I'm suffering with this spine injury....on and on and on and on....that doesn't even scratch the surface. Fact is my rage was just at me. I was enraged because I had given up and I was enraged that I had to fight to get my life back. All in all, my rage was what was keeping me alive. I needed to learn how to channel it and turn it around. I'm not some ninny hopping Easter Bunny freak happy. I'm just happy. I'm proud of myself. I'm still a little chubsy ubsy but not at all like what I used to be. My face looks like my face again. I looked like I was having an allergy attack every day. I'm a little older looking, sure. Sadly, though, I have anger lines instead of laugh lines. My forehead looks like loose leaf paper and the line between them could easily pass for a canyon. When I smile with my mouth closed, I'm actually frowning. So, I've learned how to move my scalp and wiggle my ears (yes, that's true) so I don't look like a

forehead monster and when I smile, boy, I smile with all

teeth. I put my shoulders back so in every picture I look

almost ridiculously proud...because I am.


Stay here with me, my friend. If I made you laugh or I

made you think, remember which part did that. Dog leaf

the page and hear me telling you that I think the world is

a hell of a lot better with you in it. And if no one told you

yet today, I love you. I believe in you. I know you have

something in you that's better than this. I know you can

get up and tell me you WILL because you CAN! You are a

blessing and you belong here. All of us are going to die

at some point but, we have a contract. This is a contract

we cannot breach. You have a seat in whatever heaven

is for you already reserved. Why rush it? When you close

this book, you say, out loud, "I CAN!" Because, darling, I

know you can.


Didn't we have fun?

Surely I have way more people to thank than this. To

anyone whose name is not actually written, know that

it's carved somewhere on this beating heart.

And so my friends....


It is with a certain kind of sadness that I realize, at some

point, we have to come to a close for now. I could

continue to write daily and then you'd have a 1200 page

epic while still getting 1201, 1202, 1203.....etc. in the

mail daily. Like a subscription if you will. I wouldn't even know how to begin to wrap up the years I've given away. So much has happened and basically you were right along with me for the ride. Maybe I'll make new friends. I'm positive that I'll meet new enemies. 12 billion people can tell you they love it. One person could say it sucked....and we all know who would suck the life out of me. Eh, can't win'em all kid.

These days I'm a Certified Alcohol and Substance Abuse Counselor as well as a Recovery Coach. I am the Chairperson for The Peer Recovery Network and I also teach Recovery Coaches. I am a project coordinator for a Telephone Recovery Support. I have irreplaceable relationships with my bosses and my coworkers as well as colleagues. My opinion is respected  and asked for.

My suggestions are taken more often than not. I stay

late at work if the boss tells me to go home because I'm

not finished what I need done. Who in the hell does

that?! I seem to always have a soul train behind me to

ask questions, file complaints, advocate for them,

change their diaper, shine there new cowboy boots,

make them a cup o'noodle...now I don't do these things

because I'm kissing ass, I'm doing it because I love what I

do. God spared me one last time and shook me and said,

"You listen to me, little sister, I gave you some pretty

decent talents. I'll admit, I'm a little annoyed with you

that you would pack it in so quickly and just leave those

talents to rest inside that wooden box with you. You

fought your way back, though, so my decision is to make

them a little more noticeable. When you asked that

nurse to help you in the hospital because you knew

you'd have trouble making it, I knew I'd need to pull out

the "big guns" and surround you by people who would

tell you that you're smart, you're worth having around.

That you're helpful, that you have the ability to make

someone laugh when they were sure they couldn't.

Most of all, you knew their pain was very real because

you had and felt that same pain.


So here I am today, using the talents God gave me every

day all day as a way for me to not only thank Him but to

thank the people around me who believed in me. Now I

realize I have to write an accolade page and for me to

have to thank everyone who helped me get here seems

almost impossible. The nurse when I was in ICU after

almost throwing myself the pity party of a lifetime who would act angry every time she came in to check my machines..until one day when she realized I was pretty coherent, she told me that I was beautiful and she told me I was worth more than this because she could see it in my eyes. She told me to toughen up and get out of there. Every day after that,when she came in to check on me,she stopped by my bed for a second, in silence and who'd hold my hand and pat it with her other hand. The day they moved me it of ICU, she wasn't at work so I didn't get to thank her. I was so out of it while I was in there, I don't even know her name. I tried going back there once and when I explained who I was looking for, they all looked at me like I was nuts so I wonder, still to this day, was she real or was she an angel who begged me to wake up. To Jennifer Peteroy nee Blandino who has been my best friend since I was 14 years old, who I woke up to while being hooked up to every machine possible, holding my hand with tears streaming down her face asking me, "why?" And every day that I was in there, I'd wake up to her red face with clear streams running through her makeup to show me more tears that she shed but tried to hide just to be strong enough to make life normal again by bringing me things like blueberry muffins from Dunkin Donuts. For that fact that she pulled up in front of my house a half hour before I needed to leave to take me to the most frightening psych ward you'll ever see, to make sure that they were going to send me someplace to make me safe from that point forward. I chose to do full time outpatient because she was there, otherwise she would have gone into the room with the person doing my assessment and lifted her up by her throat to make sure I did choose to go full time. She held my hand and she smiled and said, "I know everything is going to be ok, Sari." To you Jenn, who brings God to me every day. For standing by me when no one else would. For being the kind of best friend everyone in life only ever dreams of.

To the woman who did do my assessment and fought me on the idea of me telling her I didn't have an alcohol problem, I was just flat out crazy on my own. She side eyed me until I said, "fine *in spoiled brat tone* I'll give it a shot."

To the first asshole who did my outpatient intake and announced to the entire waiting room on my first day, one of the more personal if not fascinating parts of my life because he thought it was fabulously juicy. He also made a habit it of sexually harassing every young girl who walked in there and complaints were filed and yet still, there he continues to work. Why do I thank him?

Because he brought me to Vicki, who became my therapist. And it almost makes me said to just refer to her as my therapist, because Vicki is a caped crusader in my world. She knew exactly when to tell me to cut the shit. She knew exactly when to invite me to stop saying cliche's like, "I just want her to be happy." By saying things like, "Right,Sar....you want someone who makes you cry regularly, who's broken your heart fairly regularly....to be happy? How about we just leave it at, "I don't really wish her anything. Not good, not bad...just

nothing. You've given enough of your strength to

someone who gives you minimal strength. It took me a

very long time to get to that place but, I finally did begin

to understand what she meant and why it made so

much sense. Vicki, who put herself, in her beautiful

clothes, onto the floor and held my sweaty head in her

lap...one hand cradling my face while I felt her thumb

running across my cheek while she first, very sternly,

told everyone to please get out of the room and then

soothingly kept repeating to me, "ok, see...it's time now.

Time to just get it all out and let it go. It's all going to get

better now...." She cradled and rocked me in that filthy

floor - ran her hand across my drenched head without

even a second thought. She she held meat my scariest

until I was right. And let me tell ya, Vicki's a little

woman....but I wouldn't wanna be in the wrong side of the alley she's walking down. As far as I'm concerned, Vicki isn't even human. She tucks her wings into her shirt every morning and fights this good fight with the kind of inner strength I have never known and that I will always try to remember when I have my scarier moments in this field. I could write a book alone on all of this things that Vicki has taught me, done for me, done with me. What I've seen her do for other people. You know, when you're the kind of spoiled brat I am, and someone had enough confidence and knows you well enough to respond with things like, "maybe one day you'll realize the whole world doesn't revolve around you." And you don't get angry but, you rather take the advice and apply it to life, you've met your match with your therapist. I do, these days, consider Vicki to be an amazing friend.

We no longer see or talk to one another on a

therapeutic level but, will occasionally catch up on life. I

respect her opinion and any time, which happens at

least once a day, I feel like I need to tell her that I

applied something she had taught me in my work and,

well, it worked. Bumper stickers are being

made...WWVD (What would Vicki do) because. If you're

gonna be in this field, find a mentor who knock your

socks off. Try not to make it, however, someone who is

really uncomfortably attractive because then you have

to start learning about transference and counter

transference and that's just another chapter altogether.

(Yes, I did partially believe that I was in love with her.

Realize this...I'm a somewhat disheartened, single, a

little bit older lesbian. I come face to face with someone

who is not only brilliant in just about any topic you bring

up but listens to the deepest, darkest, scariest recesses of your brain and never once makes you feel weird. She recommends you for things and when she talks with you, she laughs. When you cry, she responds. She didn't leave her outpatient center too much earlier than I did. I believe she had left about 4 months before I completed. Transference and counter transference without getting too clinical, basically means someone you're dealing with professionally could remind you of a person you might love, hate, have unresolved issues with, are attracted to, etc. could maybe remind you of a family member an old friend...you get the gist. Now,this goes both ways. Sometimes you might remind the therapist of someone and that could hinder your progress. Vicki, aesthetically, looks like an ex of mine. One that did not have a good ending or hold the most fantastic corners of my mind. So, I know that when I saw Vicki, my plan was to really eat her alive. Manipulate her to death. Boy, did that girl get my number quick. I don't think I could have sold that woman mittens in the dead of winter during a mandatory snowball fight. The confusion is this; Vicki now became an improved version of my ex. I had already been incredibly physically attracted to my ex but, her personality left much to be desired. Now, I basically have this perfect woman in front of me. She's extraordinarily intelligent, book wise and weird fact wise. She's small in stature but carries herself like a bull. And I mean that in a way where, yes, she's small and very feminine but she has a way of carrying herself where you know, beyond a shadow of a doubt, to not mess with her. She's funny and she doesn't keep herself from laughing or even crying for that matter. She obviously doesn't mind getting her hands dirty - she'd

either smile to reassure me or give me that "yeah right"

lip pucker head nod. (Give yourself a minute to

understand the facial expression I just tried to explain) -

she told me off when I needed to be and humbled me

when I was far too arrogant for my own good. On top of

all of these fabulous traits, she's ridiculously attractive

and a woman who holds all of those attributes should

not be allowed out of the house. Ok, now that I'm done

embarrassing her, the real fact of the matter is, I

wouldn't be quite where I am today without Vicki's

brilliance, patience, belief, tears, laughter....all of the

amazing things she helped me find inside of myself. I

absolutely pray that anyone who does want professional

help can get someone who is even a fraction of the all

star I had. If your therapist was even half the person

mine was, then you have an unbelievably extraordinary therapist. Vicki, for each time we just nodded at each other when my session was done, I became a better woman. And for what it's worth, in the most platonic way I can possibly say this...you are the first love of my new life. Thank you for "told you so". Because apparently I believed you and became the woman you thought I could be.

Diana...you keep me humble and never pull any punches with me. You keep me honest and have a wonderful knack for getting on my nerves for being right. Every time I see you, it's "tomorrow" no matter how long it's been. You hang onto my text rants that make no sense, so in essence, you allow me to still drunk text when I'm completely sober. Your smile and your laugh ground me and make me fly all at the same time. To have found you this late in life and have you here the way you are, makes me believe I've known you in every other life..and I just wait around in the new one to find you. You bring out the fighter and the believer in me. I admire you in so many ways, I wouldn't even know where to begin. Platonically, (so funny that I have to continuously write platonic..clearly that's an issue) I fall in love with you over and over because you bring out the best in me.

DeeDe you ARE my Recovery Coach.

To the Dona/Donna's - you gave me something I could finally be proud of. You offered me an opportunity to be something great. To prove myself. In a speech I had given at my graduation, I explained these three women, Donna Nelson, Dona Pagan and Donna Mae DePola as the Dona/Donna's of Oz. When I was brave enough to pull back the curtain, I found 3 incredible women who gave me an unbreakable heart, an unbeatable brain and extraordinary courage. Remember these three names I tell you because they are the 3 most brilliant women on this earth. To work for them, to work with them, to be any part of them is the finest reward for this fight I could have ever been given. To have been chosen by these women to be part of this company is a gift from God. One I will be eternally grateful for. Ladies, you bring out the very best in my fight. You shine a light on what I'm capable of. You believe in me, you talk to me and you trust me. Donna Pagan, you once said to me, "Sarah, water seeks it's own level!" Considering the company I'm in, ladies, I am a tsunami. My respect for you has no words and no limits. Thank you for believing in me.

Christina you have stood by me, laughed at my jokes, protected me like a lioness would her cub. You've loved me through thick and thin and have made memories with me that last beyond a lifetime. No matter how far we go, we always come together again and that makes you eternal. I wear my St. Christina medal (and yes, I know St. Christina protected crazy people which can't be a bad thing draped around my neck) because she represents you to me. Someplace safe. Someplace where I am always home.

Stef, just when I thought I knew everything...I meet a friend who asks me so many damn questions without even so much as an ounce of filtration, I figure...better write a book. I never knew I was nearly as fascinating as you made me feel. Seemed like everything I had done up until the point of meeting you was just what it was. No real meaning, no real purpose. Just life. We've fought a good fight, my friend. People all but tortured you, lied to and about you, put you down and turned their back on you because of me. Underneath the weirdness and the tortured mind you were dealing with, you threw on your spelunking helmet and kept on digging. If I told you that I believed beagles were the source of global warming, you'd grab a bubble tea, pull up a seat and ask me why. Not only would you listen to the whole maniacal scenario, you would add to it and debate me. Suddenly I really knew everything that had gone on in my life was not just "whatever". I found a kind of strength in me, through you, that I never knew I had. I don't think I would have weathered what you had to. You stood shoulder to shoulder with me through malicious gossip and horrible intentions because it was just enough for you to know the truth and not worry what everyone else thought. That's a tough character, girl! When our friendship first began, as is the case in every new relationship, there was so much we wanted to know about the other. You, my very best, we're relentless. It definitely hasn't been an easy road but as bad as I got, you always seemed to find some kind of good in there. It was like going into a hoard of trash to find a treasure. Nothing expensive or frilly...just one little treasure buried under a lot of dangerous junk. The start of this relationship came with fiery texting. Question after question after question about my nonsensical life. Forcing me to understand why I was. Who I was. Where I was. And at a time when you couldn't ask the questions fast enough and I couldn't answer them fast enough, you sent me the last text, "Wanna go live?" Which meant why don't we verbally speak instead of texting. Something all of us seldom do these days. But it was so much deeper than that. That one question ran so much deeper than "let's talk". It meant, "I want to hear you. I want to feel the words and know what they mean. I want to know what makes you tick. Do you laugh? Do you cry? Do you scream? Do you hear the wonderful, absurd, intelligent, ridiculous, sad, happy......do you hear your own self and your own story?" From that moment forward, that has been the reason. Because every single day, since you've asked me that question, in every single way, I will always be "Going Live".

To my mother who I knew would be my most honest critic. I handed her the first printed version of this book and she sat down in the living room and read a little at a time and told me every night when I came home....that she loved it. So, if any of you are closing this book with a sense of enjoyment, you have my mother to thank because if she shrugged her shoulders or just seemed generally unmoved, I would have never had the balls to publish this. She did, however, make me remove any kind of sex stuff. I mean, she is my mother and all. What mother really wants to hear about things like, "well, who's the man in bed?" It was bad enough I explained that occasionally I threw some snippet of my sex life in there and just always hoped they had enough sense to disappear on their own when my mother read this. My mother is the reason I'm alive...she's the reason I'm starting this new, wonderful life. She listens to me and understands why I cry. She laughs hard enough at me to slap the table in front of her. She's calm and yes, maybe even almost too damn calm but it's a balance. Before I got sober, my mother, my best friend and truly the one person in life I absolutely trust told me that I scared her. That my behavior was so unhinged and volatile, that I scared her and that is one of the most awful, life altering things I've ever heard. But even in her fear, she never stopped holding me, she never stopped checking in me, she never stopped listening to me no matter how absurd and nonsensical my words or stories were. I had one bright shining moment to stand in front of a large

ceremony, have my mother stand up in a spotlight to

thank her and get her the standing ovation she deserves.

And that is a moment I will cherish always. To be able to

tell people in my world and share it with their world that

my mother is the reason I'm still alive and getting better

every day is something I could only dream of. It was a

perfect moment in time for both of us. Not many people

get a golden opportunity to really show someone how

grateful you are for them and make other people

understand the importance of you. I call my mother

myama....it doesn't sound like MY...it's kind of like

mew...the yuh sound. It's incredibly difficult, I'm finding,

to explain how to say it. I any event, when I see my

mother, no matter where we are, who's around or how

we're feeling....I will yell (and yes, frequently startle her enough to say, "Ooh you FUCK!" I seem to always bring

out the sailor in my mother)

MMMYYAAAAMMMMMAAAAAA!!!!! Because

everywhere my mother is, she deserves an introduction.

Mom, I love you...more than anyone or anything. Thank

you for being my number one fan....because I am

definitely yours!



I am an encyclopedic genius because of my father. I used

to blurt answers out to the most absurd questions and

have reasons for who, what, when, where and why and

absolutely NEVER know why I knew this information. I

would often refer to myself as a beacon of useless

information. As I got older and my father and I grew

closer, I was amazed at how incredibly intelligent my

father is. If there is ever anything I need an answer to, no matter how weird the question, my father knows the answer. If it's 1:17am and my father walks in with Pathmark bags filled with a loaf of bread...a container of milk....and a stick o' butter (that's a fun reference maybe some of you will get) and I'm sitting in the living room and he's kinda flying by to out the bags down and I randomly say, in a very monotone almost unassuming way, "dad, who played Carrie's mother?" By the time his keys hit the table, he would have already blurted out, "Piper Laurie" before I'm even really finished with question. I think my father is really one of the last remaining few "nice guys" there are in the world. Everyone on Staten Island, in some way shape or form knows my father. And yes, I have made my father somewhat famous on Facebook. It's very difficult to have the snow, the impromptu stops to "HIT IT!", the way he enjoys bread, just the all around unique way my father does his thing, and not share it with the world. It's all way too good to keep behind closed doors. Wherever I am, if I see a familiar face, after someone has said hello to me, they will immediately ask if my parents are there because they want to see them live an in person. Local celebrities. My father will always tell me how nice my friends are when they see or meet him. I'm surprised they don't tell him they love him before closing out the conversation. Dad, I love you. Thank you for every lit bit of knowledge I didn't even realize I had. It's because of you that I know in this life...nothing is ever really too serious to not find laughter somewhere in it.

Artie and Tracy...you I have to thank the most. You have given me the 3 greatest gifts I could have ever been given in your children. I often wonder about when they're old enough to read this book, which I figure would be somewhere in their mid 40's or long after I'm gone so I never need to look in any of their eyes knowing they just discovered who I really am....no, no, scratch that. Who I really was. They bring me the truest joy and have shown me that true love really does exist. From the very time I've seen each be of their faces, I truly knew that the concept of "love at first sight" exists. Often I'm asked, and quite a bit by them, why I'm not married and don't have any kids. Well, the marriage thing would have to come with a whole plethora of explanations I refuse to delve into and the kids...well, I have them. They are my kids and the most important part of my world and why I'm happy to be alive and well. To watch them grow

is like watching a miracle happen every single day.

To the three of you

No words could ever describe the love I feel for you.

There is nothing in this world I wouldn't do and nowhere

I wouldn't go for all of you. The 3 days you have all

entered my life, were the greatest days of my life and

they always will. I celebrate the love I'm capable of

feeling when I look at all of you. One day, when you've

read this book, after we've all checked your id's, you'll

have questions and you'll want to talk. Maybe you'll cry

at some things and laugh at others. Maybe some of it

will shock you and maybe some of it won't. The point is,

this is a way for you to really know who I am and who

you have in your corner. Know that you always have me.

That you can come to me with anything and positively

never be judged. That I will hold you when you cry,

protect you when you're down, always tell you how

proud I am of all of you and how I always have your

backs. My world starts and ends with you and you can't

imagine how grateful I am that for every time I've

slipped and lost my balance, I got back up. Know that

that is ALWAYS because of you. My three true loves.

www.ingramcontent.com/pod-product-compliance
Lightning Source LLC
LaVergne TN
LVHW011216080426
835509LV00005B/146